THE LIFEGUARD'S LOCKER

A parent/teacher manual for
Jump In:
A Workbook for
Reluctant and Eager Writers

Sharon Watson

Illustrations by Brett Sempsrott
Brett Sempsrott's illustrations digitized by Megan Whitaker
Cover design by Kim Williams

ISBN 13: 978-1-93012-75-0

Copyright © 2006 Sharon Watson
Fourth Printing November, 2010
Published by Apologia Educational Ministries, Inc.
1106 Meridian Plaza, Suite 220
Anderson, IN 46016
888-524-4724
www.apologia.com

Table of Contents

Table of Contents for the *Jump In* Student Text
(provided for reference)

Dear Parent and Teacher,

I wish I could sit down and talk with you about the rich subject of writing. Since that is not possible, I will have to settle for making a list. May God, whose words are life, bless your work.

1. This workbook is for middle school students. High school students who have had little practice in writing or who are reluctant writers will also find it helpful.
2. You will need to use a student-friendly grammar book in addition to this workbook (see Grammar Resources, pages 55-56).
3. There is enough teaching material in here for at least **two years**. The 10-Minute Writing Plunges will take one year; the student section will take at least another. Avoid running both programs concurrently. Teachers successfully have used the Plunges as breaks between the chapters, though, like a calming stretch between races.
4. The student workbook section has more than 240 days of material and work, including the longer assignments. Choose what you want your students to learn. You are the best judge.
5. Chapter headings labeled "The Basics" are **prerequisites** for the rest of the persuasion and exposition chapters.
6. Each day's work is labeled a *Skill*. Each skill has a **Now it's your turn** section that will take 5 to 20 minutes to complete.
7. At the end of some chapters or skills, students will pause to work on a longer assignment that may take anywhere from two to ten days to complete.
8. Each of these longer assignments has a suggested writing schedule, making it easy for you and your students to plan.
9. When students are through with the longer assignment, they may return to the *Skill* days.
10. Because a reluctant writer is more likely to write his opinion than a report, the student workbook begins with opinions and persuasion rather than exposition.
11. This workbook teaches a *Chicago*-style bibliography to simplify the process but MLA parenthetical notations and in-text citations for clarity. For writers of this age, it is important to focus on skills and practice, not on a certain association's style.
12. In order to avoid the pesky and cumbersome pronouns *he/she* and *he or she*, I use the generic *he* most often (apologies to female students).

Jump In Objectives

I. The Course

1. To develop an age-appropriate competence in all four areas of writing: persuasion, exposition, description, and narration.
2. To make writing accessible by using incremental steps in the teaching process.
3. To provide exposure to and practice in persuasion, exposition, description, narration, and poetry.
4. To provide grade-appropriate examples of good writing in order to encourage, inspire, and instruct the student.
5. To foster successful writing by breaking down the process into smaller pieces before giving the student the larger assignment.
6. To reinforce lessons by a student's response in the Now It's Your Turn sections.
7. To balance a difficult assignment by keeping the word count low.
8. To foster creativity and imagination needed for descriptive and narrative writing.
9. To engage the student by employing a conversational tone in the text.

II. Attitudes

1. To foster a love for writing by a series of small successes.
2. To dismantle a fear of writing in reluctant writers.
3. To encourage an interest in writing by beginning with opinions and persuasion.
4. To delight fearful writers by allowing them to write on a guided topic for 10 minutes without being assessed or graded (the 10-Minute Writing Plunges).
5. To encourage eager writers by providing interesting assignments.

III. Skills

1. To gain competence in writing persuasively by learning and practicing the Do List and by learning and avoiding the Don't List.
2. To develop organizational skills needed for taking notes, organizing notes, and writing essays or reports.
3. To practice organizational skills such as brainstorming and using the cluster method.
4. To learn to communicate clearly by following step-by-step instructions and by organizing before writing.
5. To develop thinking skills by completing assignments such as cause and effect, and compare and contrast.
6. To practice beginning in the body of a composition in order to disarm the fear of writing.
7. To strengthen proofreading skills by using the Mistake Medic, a self-guided proofreading tool.
8. To further writing skills in accomplished writers by assigning challenging and interesting work.
9. To strengthen skills needed for real-life writing by completing such assignments as a letter to a librarian, a newspaper article, and a how-to paper.
10. To develop a greater skill in the hidden intricacies of descriptive writing.
11. To practice skills in capturing the reader's attention, whether in fiction or nonfiction.
12. To practice writers' devices such as dovetailing, compare and contrast, hooks, and patterns of three.
13. To evaluate other writers' work, thereby learning how to critique one's own.

The **Assignments**

In any of the opinion, persuasion, or exposition chapters, students have a choice of assignments listed below. In "Description," "Narration," and "Poetry," they will accomplish most, if not all, of the assignments. Minimum word counts are included, where needed.

Opinions—You've Got Them choices (at least 150 words):
☐ Finish the opinion you began in the chapter.
☐ Write your opinion of writing.
☐ Write your opinion of an animal you like.
☐ Write your opinion from the favorite/worst lists.
☐ Write your opinion on something you feel strongly about.

Persuasion: The Basics choices (at least 200 words):
☐ Finish the persuasive paper you began in the chapter.
☐ Write a persuasive paper on a topic you feel strongly about.
☐ Write a letter to a librarian about a great/horrible video or book.

Persuasion: Cause and Effect choices (at least 250 words):
☐ Finish the cause and effect paper you began in this chapter.
☐ Write about an invention and its good or bad effects on the world.
☐ Choose something other than an invention and write about its good or bad effects.

Exposition: The Basics choices (at least 300 words):
☐ Write a report on an animal you love. Include a bibliography.
☐ Write a report on an animal you can't stand. Include a bibliography.
☐ Write a report on a country you want to visit. Include a bibliography.
☐ Write a report on a subject of interest to you. Include a bibliography.

Exposition: A Biography choices (at least 300 words):
☐ Write a simple chronological biography.
☐ Write a biography using one of the eight ways to write one.
☐ Write a biography of your creation.
☐ Write your autobiography.

Exposition: A Book Report choices (at least 300 words):
☐ Write a book report on a favorite book. Use the Book Report Form.
☐ Write a book report on a book you don't like. Use the Book Report Form.
☐ Write a book report on a book your teacher assigns you. Use the Book Report Form.

Exposition: A Book Response choices (variable):
☐ Complete an artistic-skill book response.
☐ Complete a writing-skill book response.
☐ Complete a new book response that you invent.

Exposition: A Newspaper Article choices (200-300 words):
☐ Finish the news article you began in this chapter.
☐ Choose a Bible (or other) story and write it as a newspaper article.

Exposition: A How-to choices (100-300 words):
☐ Write a how-to in the Essay Method.
☐ Write a how-to in the Instruction Manual Method.

Exposition: Compare and Contrast choices:
☐ Beginning writers: Write a paragraph to compare and contrast two people, objects, or elements of nature (approx. 100 words).
☐ Experienced writers: Write a paper to compare and contrast two items, people, places, events, and so forth (at least 300 words).

Description
☐ Write a description of one bird out of 19.
☐ Make a dull paragraph interesting.
☐ Find similes.
☐ Find metaphors.
☐ Record sensory experiences.
☐ Put a fictional character into the place you recorded (at least 100 words).
☐ Write a paragraph describing a room (at least 100 words).
☐ Write a paragraph describing a person (at least 100 words).
☐ Write a paragraph describing a scene (at least 100 words).
☐ Imitate a paragraph.

Narration (Storytelling)
☐ Write a 10-minute story using four unrelated items.
☐ Write hooks; write 10-minute stories from the hooks.
☐ Write a story putting a fictional character into another setting (at least 300 words).
☐ Create a character.
☐ Write a paragraph describing your character's favorite place (at least 100 words).
☐ Write a situation to show your character's major trait (at least 250 words).
☐ Identify points of view.
☐ Write Daniel 2 from someone else's point of view (at least 250 words).
☐ Write someone's motivation.
☐ Resolve a conflict from a scenario (at least 300 words).
☐ Write new dialogue for characters in a movie scene (3 pages).
☐ Write a dialogue between two people who are stuck in an elevator (at least 200 words).
☐ Write a fable (at least 200 words).
☐ Identify patterns of three.
☐ Write a fairy tale, tall tale, parable, and so forth (at least 300 words).
☐ Optional: Choose a story from the list and write it.

Poetry
☐ Write a haiku.
☐ Write a cinquain.
☐ Write a diamante.
☐ Write a limerick.
☐ Write a hymn.
☐ Imitate a poem.
☐ Write a new set of lyrics for a song.

Why a Reluctant Writer Hates to Write and What You Can Do About It!

1. He received negative feedback in earlier grades that discouraged him.

☞ Evaluate his work by using the grading section that begins on page 17. Point out what he does well.

2. His strengths lie elsewhere: math, science, working with his hands, sports, relationships, music, and so forth.

☞ Tap into his strengths and interests. He can write his opinion on why everyone should be smart in math. Tie writing to science by assigning him a short report on a topic of interest to him. A kinesthetic student can write a how-to on something he knows how to do. Your sports lover can write a play-by-play of an exciting part of a game or write instructions on how to play a sport. A relationship-oriented student can write with a friend, write an advice column, or compose essays on friendship or the perils of gossiping. A musician can describe how it feels like to play music.

3. He believes that writing is a secret art with no discernable rules into which he must enter with a secret password he doesn't have.

☞ Teach him the very specific ideas and patterns in this book. Buy a grammar book that he understands (see Grammar Resources, pages 55, 56). Go over the **Mistake Medic** on page 14 with him. Demystify writing. The passwords are *learn* and *practice*.

4. He doesn't have enough time to think about and write his assignments.

☞ Allow him enough time to perform these separate operations: brainstorming, writing, and proofreading. Help him plan a schedule for each new assignment. *Writing takes time; good writing takes even more!*

5. He is a perfectionist who forces himself to have everything in order (including his thoughts) before he will write.

☞ Teach him how to brainstorm and make lists of ideas or points *on paper* so he can arrange them later in the order in which he wants them. Immerse him in the **10-Minute Writing Plunges**, which will allow him to write *without being graded on everything he writes.*

6. Earlier writing assignments were too difficult for him, so he gave up.

☞ Encourage him! Use the small bites and low word counts in this textbook. Ask him what is hard about writing and help him find the answers in this book or in his grammar book.

Hot Writing Tips to Help Your Young Writer

Using her spelling list, she can write a short story that includes most of the words.

Consider giving your student a small **reward** for completing a certain number of assignments. Yea! Something to look forward to!

Use the 10-Minute Writing Plunges (beginning on page 40) daily. They are short and sweet and full of inspiration. Best of all, your young writer only has to polish one of these a week. What a writing bargain!

Monitor his work by sitting at the table with him and by minimizing the distractions.

Invite your young writer to write a story with a **friend.** You will be surprised by what they create!

Choose a writing schedule and stick to it! Your student will know what to expect and won't fight the experience (or you!) as much.

Put **four unrelated objects** on the table and ask your student to write a short story that uses them (see Narration, Skill 1, page 195 and 196 in student text, for examples of this).

During the Writer's Block phase of writing, use the Interview Method with your writer. Ask questions like "Why?" and "What happens next?" and "Tell me more." The exchange with you will give him ideas.

Going on a trip or a vacation? Let your young writer buy her own journal to keep track of what she sees and does on the trip. Allow her to write in it daily but promise not to look at it. Some writing is private! Someday, however, she may use some of these experiences in her writing for school.

Writing From Beginning to End

(Students have a copy of this information in **YOUR LOCKER** on page 237.)

Brainstorm. Write down ideas. If your teacher lets you choose the topic, list things you know a lot about or are interested in. If your teacher chooses the topic, write down all the different possibilities inside this topic.

Narrow down your ideas. You can't possibly use all of them in your assignment. Keep the ones you can use and cross off the rest. Sometimes you won't know which ones to keep until you begin to research or write.

Make a list, outline, cluster, or Greek temple of all the ideas you intend to keep, putting them in a logical order for your paper.

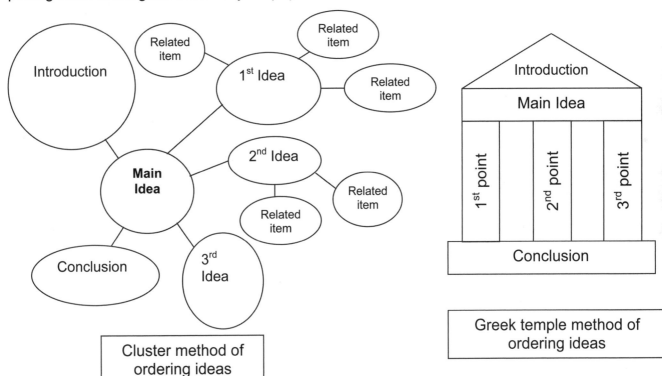

Cluster method of ordering ideas

Greek temple method of ordering ideas

Begin writing. Use the list you just made. Begin wherever you want to but remember to include an introductory paragraph, a new paragraph for each point, and a conclusion. Don't worry about mistakes. Write now; fix later. This is your first draft. Some call it a rough draft or a sloppy copy. <u>Never</u> hand this in to your teacher as your finished assignment.

Set your paper aside for a few hours or days. This means you won't be able to wait until the last minute to write it. When you set it aside, you are giving it time to cool off so that you can do the next step with a level head.

Reread your paper. By now, you will see some mechanical mistakes (commas, spelling, capitalization, and so forth). You will also notice some mistakes in how you said things. You will think of better phrases or sentences. Did you leave out a word? Did you misuse a word? You may want to move a whole sentence to another place. Maybe you will want to cross out some sentences and put others in. Fix your paper! Use **Mistake Medic** (on page 14 as well as on page 238 in the student workbook).

Proofread it. Comb through your paper. Look for all sorts of mistakes. Look for them one sentence at a time. Read your paper out loud. Resize the font. Proofread it from a printed copy, not from the screen. You will be surprised how many mistakes you find when you do these things.

Write your paper again. Make it as polished and as neat as possible. Before handing it in, read it one more time—slowly—to look for mistakes.

Hand it in and smile. If you have done all these steps well, both you and your teacher will be proud of your work.

Tips to Help Your Student Proofread

THESE ARE **CHOICES**, NOT A CHRONOLOGICAL LIST:

- Tell him to **print out each version** as he edits it, showing you the progression of his proofreading.

- Tell him to **double-space** his work and **print it off**. He will find many more mistakes this way and will have room to correct them.

- Ask to see the **outline, list, cluster, or Greek temple** he used to organize his thoughts. This makes him aware of his need to organize before he writes.

- Ask what his **topic** is. Also ask for his **main idea** or **thesis statement** for the whole paper. He should be able to sum it up in 20 words or less.

- Ask him what the **topic sentence** or **main point** is for each paragraph.

- If he is writing a story, have him **sum up the plot** in 40 words or less. *The Hobbit*, for example, could be this: The hobbit Bilbo, who hates adventures, has to take a journey to help dwarfs recover an ancient treasure from a dragon.

- Put a **check mark** next to any line that has a mistake. Then he can look for the mistake.

- Put a check mark next to any line that has a mistake and **label the mistake:** comma, question mark, missing a word or two, run-on sentence, sentence fragment, etc. Then he can find it.

- Circle the **spelling mistakes** but don't correct them. Consider including some of your student's common spelling mistakes on the next spelling test.

- At the bottom of the page, write **how many grammar and/or punctuation mistakes you found.** Then help your student find them.

- **Listen** to your student read the paper out loud. The number of mistakes he finds this way will surprise, amaze, and astound both of you. He should have his pen handy for this exercise.

- Review **Mistake Medic** (page 14) with him. He should use this for every assignment. His copy is in **YOUR LOCKER** on page 238.

Mistake Medic

1. Reread your paper:
   - Does it have an interesting title?
   - Does the opening sentence or paragraph grab the reader's attention by making a point, stating a fact, using a quotation, telling a story, or asking a question?
   - Does your paper get to the point quickly?
   - Does it stick to the point?
   - Is there a logical progression from one point to the next?

   - Is it easy to read and easy to understand?
   - Does the conclusion give the reader something interesting to think about?

2. Check your title for correct capital letters. Don't underline it or put quotation marks around it. Skip a line after the title.

3. Is your paper double-spaced?

4. Did you indent (five spaces) the first line of every paragraph?

5. Read your paper aloud. Is anything confusing? Add words or change them as necessary.

6. Look for unnecessarily repeated words. Use specific adjectives and nouns and powerful verbs, but don't get fancy.

7. Look for run-on sentences and sentence fragments.

8. Make sure all your commas are there for a reason, not just because you want to pause or have to hiccup. Check your other punctuation in the middle and at the end of sentences. Refer to your grammar book.

9. Check your capital letters. Every sentence begins with one. Every proper noun needs one.

10. Circle possible spelling mistakes and homonym mistakes (*there, their*, and *they're*, for example). Then look them up in a dictionary.

11. Try these **tricks** to catch more mistakes. You will be surprised how many more you will find:
    a. **Print your paper** instead of proofreading it at the computer screen.
    b. **Resize the font** or choose another font. This moves the words into new positions, making it easier to catch mistakes you would normally read over.
    c. **Read your paper out loud** and listen to what you are saying.
    d. **Read each word**. Don't skim.

Opinions—What to Look For

Elementary Students—writing an **opinion**

1. What is the topic? What is the student's opinion on the topic? These should be clear and appear in the first paragraph. (Simple examples: "I'm against the war in Reykjavik" or "Candy bars make great snacks.")

2. Is the first sentence interesting enough that the reader wants to keep reading?

3. Does each following paragraph (except for the conclusion) tell a new reason why your student is for the idea or against it? One reason = one paragraph.

4. In what order are the reasons/paragraphs? They should be in some sort of logical order: chronological, most important to least important, and so forth.

5. Does the last paragraph (the conclusion) restate the student's opinion in a different form, giving the reader something to think about? Does it include an interesting fact, tell a story to prove the point, and so forth?

6. Has your student written the opinion without making fun of others who believe differently? (The apostle Paul, for example, never made fun of opposing views but simply told the truth and respected his audience.)

Junior and Senior High School Students—trying to **persuade**
(**Add the following list to the above list**. After brainstorming ideas, the student should write a sentence to guide him through writing the persuasive paper: "I am going to convince the reader that…" or "I would like to persuade other teens to…." This sentence will not appear in his writing.)

1. Has the student considered the audience? Writing to peers will be different than writing to the local newspaper or the church newsletter.

2. Does the introductory paragraph begin with an interesting statement, fact, or quotation, a story to illustrate the point, or a pointed question to make the reader think? Does the conclusion give food for thought and include a call to action?

3. Has the student shown he knows both sides of the argument by respectfully mentioning an opposing view and refuting it ("Some say…, but scientists have shown that…")?

4. Has the student included not just opinions but facts to back up those opinions?

5. Has the student correctly cited his sources ("Dr. Sassafras of the DNR states…" or "According to the information on www.welovepickles.com, people would rather eat one dill pickle than ten sweet pickles")?

Grading Section

How Do I Give a Grade?

A B O V E   A L L ,   B E   E N C O U R A G I N G

→ Read the assignment for **content** first. Did the student follow the directions? Is the paper clear? Is it in a logical order? Avoid grading his opinion or ideas; grade how well he wrote his paper.

→ Next, read it for **grammar and mechanics**. Punctuation, capitalization, spelling, paragraphing, and good grammar go in this category. At these grade levels, <u>do not correct everything that is wrong.</u> Just as a new wife would quickly stop cooking if her husband graded her on all the meals she cooked, so a young writer will dry up and stop writing if he is graded on everything he writes all the time. Choose a particular focus each month or semester (commas, spelling, etc.) and grade that.

→ Give two grades for each assignment: one for the content and one for the grammar and mechanics. For the same assignment, the grades often are quite different from each other.

→ Use one of the evaluation forms on the following pages to get a better picture of the grade your student has earned. On the following pages you will find **three kinds of evaluation forms:**

- a generic form
- a guided form for nonfiction
- a guided form for fiction

Not all of the questions on the forms will apply to all assignments, so use your best judgment. Grade leniently at the beginning of the year and more strictly when you have covered the material. Over the course of this workbook, your student will have encountered all the information in the evaluation questions when you couple this book with an understandable grammar text.

You will also find **sample evaluations** for middle school students I've taught, used with their permission. Please note that *I haven't corrected everything that was wrong on those papers.* Be judicious about what you correct. Your student's papers will not be perfect. Don't aim for perfection; aim for progress.

Use your own judgment when converting circled numbers from the evaluation forms into grades. Some questions have more weight than others.

→ Make use of the special section "How to Earn an A Paper," "How to Earn a B Paper," and so forth. It breaks down how each real student earned each grade, and it uses the Writing Evaluation Form for Nonfiction.

Generic Writing Evaluation Form for Fiction or Nonfiction

STUDENT: _____

TITLE: _____

ASSIGNMENT: _____

<u>CONTENT:</u>

<u>GRAMMAR/MECHANICS:</u>

<u>ADVICE:</u>

Writing Evaluation Form for **Nonfiction**

STUDENT: _____

TITLE: _____

ASSIGNMENT: _____

CONTENT	NO	Somewhat		YES	
1. Did the student follow the assignment directions?	1	2	3	4	5
2. Does the paper begin with an interesting statement, fact, question, quote, or story?	1	2	3	4	5
3. Is the topic (subject matter) clear from reading the introductory paragraph?	1	2	3	4	5
4. Is there a clear thesis statement?	1	2	3	4	5
5. Is it near the end of the first paragraph?	1	2	3	4	5
6. Does the paper support the thesis statement?	1	2	3	4	5
7. Does the paper stick to the topic?	1	2	3	4	5
8. Are there transitions from one paragraph to the next?	1	2	3	4	5
9. Are there effective topic sentences?	1	2	3	4	5
10. Are the points clear and logical?	1	2	3	4	5
11. Are they in a logical order?	1	2	3	4	5
12. Does each point have good supporting statements?	1	2	3	4	5
13. Is the paper interesting or humorous?	1	2	3	4	5
14. Is it clear that the research was done well?	1	2	3	4	5
15. Does the paper show good use of the targeted writer's device (metaphor, transitions, etc.)?	1	2	3	4	5
16. Does the conclusion give food for thought, not just recount points?	1	2	3	4	5
17. Persuasion: Does the student follow the "Do List"?	1	2	3	4	5
18. Persuasion: Does the student avoid the "Don't List"?	1	2	3	4	5
19. Persuasion: Is there a call to action?	1	2	3	4	5

Grade_____

GRAMMAR/MECHANICS					
1. Is there an introductory paragraph?	1	2	3	4	5
2. Is there a separate paragraph for each point?	1	2	3	4	5
3. Is there a concluding paragraph?	1	2	3	4	5
4. Does the student avoid fragments except for effect?	1	2	3	4	5
5. Does the student avoid run-on sentences?	1	2	3	4	5
6. Does the student use good grammar?	1	2	3	4	5
7. Does the student avoid jargon, lingo, or slang?	1	2	3	4	5
8. If there is special jargon, is it defined?	1	2	3	4	5
9. Does the student use comma rules well?	1	2	3	4	5
10. Is the rest of the punctuation/capitalization correct?	1	2	3	4	5
11. Is the spelling correct?	1	2	3	4	5
12. Are there varying sentence structures and lengths?	1	2	3	4	5
13. Does the student correctly cite sources (reports, etc.)?	1	2	3	4	5
14. Is the paper double-spaced?	1	2	3	4	5

Check for CONTENT or GRAMMAR/MECHANICS remarks on the back.

Grade _____

Writing Evaluation Form for **Fiction**

STUDENT: _____

TITLE: _____

ASSIGNMENT: _____

CONTENT

	NO	Somewhat		YES

	NO		Somewhat		YES
1. Did the student follow the assignment directions?	1	2	3	4	5
2. Does the student use an interesting hook?	1	2	3	4	5
3. Is the conflict clear?	1	2	3	4	5
4. Does the conflict get worse before it gets better?	1	2	3	4	5
5. Does the story have an effective climax?	1	2	3	4	5
6. Is the conflict resolved in a believable way?	1	2	3	4	5
7. Are the characters believable?	1	2	3	4	5
8. Is the dialogue true to each character?	1	2	3	4	5
9. Is the plot/action interesting?	1	2	3	4	5
10. Is there a good balance between dialogue and narration (story, action, and description)?	1	2	3	4	5
11. Does the student describe the time and place of the story (the setting)?	1	2	3	4	5
12. Are there other noteworthy descriptions of people, places, or objects?	1	2	3	4	5
13. Does the story move forward without getting snagged somewhere?	1	2	3	4	5
14. Does the paper show good use of the targeted writer's device (metaphor, dialogue, etc.)?	1	2	3	4	5
15. Is there something you like about the story?	1	2	3	4	5

Grade_____

GRAMMAR/MECHANICS

	NO		Somewhat		YES
1. Does the student use good grammar?	1	2	3	4	5
2. Does the student use the comma rules well?	1	2	3	4	5
3. Are there paragraphs?	1	2	3	4	5
4. Does each speaker get a new paragraph?	1	2	3	4	5
5. Is the dialogue punctuation correct?	1	2	3	4	5
6. Is the rest of the punctuation/capitalization correct?	1	2	3	4	5
7. Is the spelling correct?	1	2	3	4	5
8. Does the student avoid fragments except for effect?	1	2	3	4	5
9. Does the student avoid run-on sentences?	1	2	3	4	5
10. Are there varying sentence structures and lengths?	1	2	3	4	5
11. Is the story double-spaced?	1	2	3	4	5

Grade _____

Check for CONTENT or GRAMMAR/MECHANICS remarks on the back.

Sample Generic Evaluation for **Nonfiction**

STUDENT: A boy in the eighth grade

TITLE: "Antique Cars"

ASSIGNMENT: Opinion, 300-word minimum (there are 301 words).

CONTENT:

I agree with you. I like the old cars better too! You have two good reasons why you like the older ones better: They are easier to work on, and they stand out. You have done a fine job of supporting your reasons. Consider using three reasons next time, and make sure that each reason gets a separate paragraph.

In the middle of your first reason (paragraph 2), you mention tires. However, this sentence doesn't seem to fit there unless you mention how easy they were to fix, change, or patch. (It is in your "easier to work on" paragraph.) If the tires were better made, make them a separate paragraph and tell us why—we want to know!

GRAMMAR/MECHANICS:

The paragraph about the cars standing out merged with your concluding paragraph. Make sure your conclusion is separate.

Check your "they're" and "their" usage. Sometimes you use the wrong one.

In lines 1, 8, and 19, you used "then" instead of "than." "Then" is a word to use with time: *Then* the car broke down. "Than" is a comparing word: I like vanilla better *than* chocolate.

Review your comma rules.

Use "today" or "modern" in place of "now a day."

Insert a dash here: "…definitely choose the old one—no doubt about it."

ADVICE:

You have a natural style that is easy to read. I hope your first car is fun to work on!

Note to teacher: Be selective about which mistakes to highlight, especially at the beginning of the writing year.

Antique Cars

Old cars were so much better then the new ones now a day. I like old cars because of the way they're made.

I like the way they're made because they're easier to work on. The engine is so much more open so that you can work on it if needed. The frame doesn't crunch together if wrecked, like the average car does now a day. The engines weren't as complicated to work on or fix. Tires were better then the ones today. Parts wouldn't brake or have to be replaced as much. They only had to have six volts instead of twelve. Their wasn't as much wiring and it wasn't as complicated.

I like the way they look because they stand out. New cars now a days are so common that they just look normal. There are so few old cars now that you hardly ever see them. When you do see them and they have been taken care of or restored they look great and they stand out. Most people like the new cars just because they're new and there what's in style. Even though old cars don't go as fast as easily or aren't as luxurious I still like them better then new one's. If you were to compare cars then and now I would say that cars back then look twice as good as the cars now a days do. If you were to look at the difference between an old car and a new one you would be able to tell pretty easily. So if I had a choice between an old car and a new car I would definitely choose the old one no doubt about it. Both old cars and new cars have their advantages and disadvantages. That is why I like old cars.

Sample Evaluation for "Antique Cars"

STUDENT: A boy in the eighth grade
TITLE: "Antique Cars"
ASSIGNMENT: Opinion of at least 300 words

CONTENT

Question	NO	Somewhat			YES
1. Did the student follow the assignment directions?	1	2	3	4	**5**
2. Does the paper begin with an interesting statement, fact, question, quote, or story?	**1**	2	3	4	5
3. Is the topic (subject matter) clear by reading the introductory paragraph?	1	2	3	4	**5**
4. Is there a clear thesis statement?	1	2	3	4	**5**
5. Is it near the end of the first paragraph?	1	2	3	4	**5**
6. Does the paper support the thesis statement?	1	2	3	4	**5**
7. Does the paper stick to the topic?	1	2	3	4	**5**
8. Are there transitions from one paragraph to the next?	**1**	2	3	4	5
9. Are there effective topic sentences?	1	2	3	4	**5**
10. Are the points clear and logical?	1	2	3	4	**5**
11. Are they in a logical order?	1	2	3	**4**	5
12. Does each point have good supporting statements?	1	2	**3**	4	5
13. Is the paper interesting or humorous?	1	2	**3**	4	5
14. Is it clear that the research was done well? N/A	1	2	3	4	5
15. Does the paper show good use of the targeted writer's device (metaphor, transitions, etc.)? [opinion paper]	1	2	3	**4**	5
16. Does the conclusion give food for thought, not just recount points?	**1**	2	3	4	5
17. Persuasion: Does the student follow the "Do List"?	1 N/A	2	3	4	5
18. Persuasion: Does the student avoid the "Don't List"?	1 N/A	2	3	4	5
19. Persuasion: Is there a call to action?	1 N/A	2	3	4	5

Grade: A-

GRAMMAR/MECHANICS

Question	NO	Somewhat			YES
1. Is there an introductory paragraph?	1	2	3	4	**5**
2. Is there a separate paragraph for each point?	1	2	**3**	4	5
3. Is there a concluding paragraph?	**1**	2	3	4	5
4. Does the student avoid fragments except for effect?	1	2	3	4	**5**
5. Does the student avoid run-on sentences?	1	2	3	4	**5**
6. Does the student use good grammar?	1	2	**3**	4	5
7. Does the student avoid jargon, lingo, or slang?	1	2	3	4	**5**
8. If there is special jargon, is it defined? N/A	1	2	3	4	5
9. Does the student use comma rules well?	1	**2**	3	4	5
10. Is the rest of the punctuation/capitalization correct?	1	2	3	**4**	5
11. Is the spelling correct?	1	2	**3**	4	5
12. Are there varying sentence structures and lengths?	1	2	**3**	4	5
13. Does the student correctly cite sources (reports, etc.)?	1 N/A	2	3	4	5
14. Is the paper double-spaced?	**1**	2	3	4	5

Grade: C

> **Note to teacher:** This was the first assignment of the year; we had not covered everything on this form yet. Therefore, the grades are lenient. If this had been later in the year, the grades would have been lower.

Sample Generic Evaluation for **Fiction**

STUDENT: A boy in the sixth grade

TITLE: "The Sly Fox and the Three Chickens"

ASSIGNMENT: Fable, 200-word minimum (there are 200 words).

CONTENT:
This is fun to read. You used a pattern of three—three times! There are three chickens, they go into the woods after the Frisbee three times, and the fox digs three holes. The "R" names are a clever idea. All of this gives the story such a nice rhythm.

The fox is sly; we know why he is mean. The chickens seem pretty gullible, even for chickens. Consider giving us the reason why they are so stupid. Did they think the fox would be a good friend? Did they listen to someone's bad advice? Were they disobeying someone? You may want to mention that the chickens ask where the food is. That will give us a hint about the ending.

Your interesting story might need a moral at the end, especially if you tell us why the chickens were so unsuspecting. Your ending, however, was very satisfying.

GRAMMAR/MECHANICS:
What can I say? You've turned in a wonderful paper! Bravo!

Think about changing the beginning of paragraph two or paragraph three. They both begin the same way.

The sentence that begins with "When they arrived at the picnic area…" could start a new paragraph because it moves the story from the barnyard to the picnic, and it describes what happens at the picnic.

ADVICE:
Keep using that great imagination!

The Sly Fox and the Three Chickens

Once upon a time a chicken named Rosie lived on a farm with her two sisters, Rachel and Renée. One day a sly fox came to the barnyard and asked them to a picnic. When they arrived at the picnic area, they threw a Frisbee to each other. Having a very strong arm, the sly fox purposely threw the Frisbee as far as he could and told the chickens to go and find it. While they were gone, the sly fox quickly dug a hole in the ground and covered it with leaves so as to disguise it from the chickens.

When Rosie, Rachel, and Renée returned with the Frisbee, the sly fox again threw the Frisbee into the woods. For a second time the three chickens went to look for the Frisbee. And again the sly fox dug another hole and covered it with leaves. Finally, the sly fox threw the Frisbee one last time into the woods. While the three chickens went to find it, the sly fox completed his last trap.

When Rosie, Rachel, and Renée returned with the Frisbee, they each fell into the sly fox's traps.   And the fox ate them all up for lunch.

Sample Evaluation for "The Sly Fox and the Three Chickens"

STUDENT: A boy in the sixth grade
TITLE: "The Sly Fox and the Three Chickens"
ASSIGNMENT: Fairy tale or fable using patterns of three, 200-word minimum

CONTENT	NO		Somewhat		YES
1. Did the student follow the assignment directions?	1	2	3	4	<u>5</u>
2. Does the student use an interesting hook?	1	2	3	4	<u>5</u>
3. Is the conflict clear?	1	2	3	4	<u>5</u>
4. Does the conflict get worse before it gets better?	1	2	3	4	<u>5</u>
5. Does the story have an effective climax?	1	2	3	4	<u>5</u>
6. Is the conflict resolved in a believable way?	1	2	3	4	<u>5</u>
7. Are the characters believable?	1	2	3	<u>4</u>	5
8. Is the dialogue true to each character? N/A	1	2	3	4	5
9. Is the plot/action interesting?	1	2	3	4	<u>5</u>
10. Is there a good balance between dialogue and narration (story, action, and description)? N/A	1	2	3	4	5
11. Does the student describe the time and place of the story (the setting)?	1	2	3	4	<u>5</u>
12. Are there other noteworthy descriptions of people, places, or objects? N/A	1	2	3	4	5
13. Does the story move forward without getting snagged somewhere?	1	2	3	4	<u>5</u>
14. Does the paper show good use of the targeted writer's device (metaphor, dialogue, etc.)? [great 3s!]	1	2	3	4	<u>5</u>
15. Is there something you like about the story?	1	2	3	4	<u>5</u>

Grade: A+

GRAMMAR/MECHANICS	NO		Somewhat		YES
1. Does the student use good grammar?	1	2	3	4	<u>5</u>
2. Does the student use the comma rules well?	1	2	3	4	<u>5</u>
3. Are there paragraphs?	1	2	3	4	<u>5</u>
4. Does each speaker get a new paragraph? N/A	1	2	3	4	5
5. Is the dialogue punctuation correct? N/A	1	2	3	4	5
6. Is the rest of the punctuation/capitalization correct?	1	2	3	4	<u>5</u>
7. Is the spelling correct?	1	2	3	4	<u>5</u>
8. Does the student avoid fragments except for effect?	1	2	3	4	<u>5</u>
9. Does the student avoid run-on sentences?	1	2	3	4	<u>5</u>
10. Are there varying sentence structures and lengths?	1	2	3	4	5 ←
11. Is the story double-spaced? [Yes, in the original.]	1	2	3	4	<u>5</u>

Not
taught
yet

Grade: A+

How to Earn an A Paper

Grading papers can be tricky and—yes—sometimes even subjective. By using the objective Writing Evaluation Forms for both fiction and nonfiction, you can smooth some of the subjectivity out of your grading and give a fair grade. These forms also take some of the burden off you and put it squarely where it should be—on the student!

Below is a biography written by a fifth-grade girl, who definitely earned an A. It appears in its original form. Read the paper and the following comments to find out what makes this an A paper.

A Cellist of Conscience

"I will tell you what I will do to him if I catch him. I will cut off his arms both of them at the elbows." This was the threat made by General Gonzalo Queipo de Llano to Pablo over the radio in 1936. His threats were dismissed and Pablo continued his stand against the Spanish Fascists.

Pablo was a small man in stature, born to Carlos and Pilar of Catalonia, Spain in 1876. Even though Carlos was a great conductor and led the local church choir, he did not want his son to grow up to be a musician. He knew that he could not earn enough money to support a family; only the best of the best could obtain wealth. However, for Pablo, musical notes were as familiar as words. He studied the piano with his father and by the age of six was playing simpler pieces of Beethoven, Mendelssohn, Chopin, and Bach. He longed to learn how to play the organ, but his father would not let him begin until his feet could reach the pedals. This took longer than most children because Pablo in adulthood only stood five feet and three inches tall.

Later, in 1885 a band of traveling musicians came through town. Pablo became fascinated by an instrument he had never seen before. It was made with a broom handle and strung like a cello, although he had never seen or heard of a cello before. He ran home and told his father that he wanted one. Carlos and Pilar were very poor. Therefore, Carlos agreed to make an instrument like the one he had seen. They made it from a long slender gourd and after a few minutes of playing it, he played a tune by Schubert. Immediately, he fell in love with this homemade instrument. It was not until he was eleven that he first heard a real cello being played. He then longed to learn how to play it. He began holding his violin like a cello between his legs instead of tucked under his chin. His father was outraged, but his mother insisted that he have the chance to study the cello.

Pablo eventually obtained a cello. When he was seventeen years old he played for the Queen of Madrid and in 1896 he played at the royal palace in Portugal. He was awarded a grant to study the cello at the Madrid Conservatory of Music. He soon became the greatest cellist in the world. He used to play his cello for political reasons. For many decades he refused to play his cello publicly for any government that supported the Fascist government of Spain. He eventually had to live in exile in Puerto Rico. In 1971 Pablo composed and performed a hymn for the United Nations.

Pablo Casals, called Pau, meaning peace, suffered from a heart attack in 1973 and died. He will always be remembered as the "Cellist of Conscience."

CONTENT:

This gal does everything right. She begins with an interesting quotation that pulls the reader into the biography. She tells the story of Pablo Casals in a clear, chronological way, beginning with his early life, continuing through to the genesis of his love of the cello, and on to his fame and political life. The reader can feel the longing Pablo must have felt as he watched his poor father craft a musical instrument for him to play. It is clear that Pablo developed not only musical talents but political convictions as well. The student ties the end to the beginning by writing about Pablo's convictions in both.

An older student would have developed the theme of Pablo's political conscience, including the people and events that shaped his views. However, for a fifth-grade paper, this student's work is admirable.

GRAMMAR/MECHANICS:

There is an introduction and conclusion. Each paragraph contains specific information about Pablo in a chronological way, stepping from paragraph to paragraph as the musician grows older.

There are a few comma mistakes that are quite normal for a fifth-grade student. For example, here are some corrections:

- "I will cut off his arms, both of them, at the elbows."
- …born to Carlos and Pilar of Catalonia, Spain, in 1876.
- …he played for the queen of Madrid, and in 1896 he played at the royal palace in Portugal.

This student uses implied topic sentences. For instance, the subject of paragraph three is definitely how Pablo's love of the cello began. She uses the transition words *later* and *eventually* in paragraphs three and four to move the topic forward.

Turn the page to see how this fifth-grade biography writer measures up in terms of the evaluation form for nonfiction.

CONTENT

	NO	Somewhat		YES
1. Did the student follow the assignment directions?	1	2	3	4	<u>5</u>
2. Does the paper begin with an interesting statement, fact, question, quote, or story?	1	2	3	4	<u>5</u>
3. Is the topic (subject matter) clear by reading the introductory paragraph?	1	2	3	<u>4</u>	5
4. Is there a clear thesis statement? [implied in quote]	1	2	3	<u>4</u>	5
5. Is it near the end of the first paragraph?	1	2	3	4	<u>5</u>
6. Does the paper support the thesis statement?	1	2	<u>3</u>	4	5
7. Does the paper stick to the topic?	1	2	<u>3</u>	4	5
8. Are there transitions from one paragraph to the next?	1	2	3	4	<u>5</u>
9. Are there effective topic sentences? [implied]	1	2	3	4	<u>5</u>
10. Are the points clear and logical?	1	2	3	4	<u>5</u>
11. Are they in a logical order?	1	2	3	4	<u>5</u>
12. Does each point have good supporting statements?	1	2	3	4	<u>5</u>
13. Is the paper interesting or humorous?	1	2	3	4	<u>5</u>
14. Is it clear that the research was done well?	1	2	3	4	<u>5</u>
15. Does the paper show good use of the targeted writer's device (metaphor, transitions, etc.)? [a biography]	1	2	3	4	<u>5</u>
16. Does the conclusion give food for thought, not just recount points?	1	2	3	4	<u>5</u>
17. Persuasion: Does the student follow the "Do List"?	1 N/A	2	3	4	5
18. Persuasion: Does the student avoid the "Don't List"?	1 N/A	2	3	4	5
19. Persuasion: Is there a call to action?	1 N/A	2	3	4	5

Grade: A+

GRAMMAR/MECHANICS

	NO	Somewhat		YES
1. Is there an introductory paragraph?	1	2	3	4	<u>5</u>
2. Is there a separate paragraph for each point?	1	2	3	4	<u>5</u>
3. Is there a concluding paragraph?	1	2	3	4	<u>5</u>
4. Does the student avoid fragments except for effect?	1	2	3	4	<u>5</u>
5. Does the student avoid run-on sentences?	1	2	3	4	<u>5</u>
6. Does the student use good grammar?	1	2	3	4	<u>5</u>
7. Does the student avoid jargon, lingo, or slang?	1	2	3	4	<u>5</u>
8. If there is special jargon, is it defined? N/A	1	2	3	4	5
9. Does the student use comma rules well?	1	2	<u>3</u>	4	5
10. Is the rest of the punctuation/capitalization correct?	1	2	3	4	<u>5</u>
11. Is the spelling correct?	1	2	3	4	<u>5</u>
12. Are there varying sentence structures and lengths?	1	2	3	4	<u>5</u>
13. Does the student correctly cite sources (reports, etc.)?	1 N/A	2	3	4	<u>5</u>
14. Is the paper double-spaced?	<u>1</u>	2	3	4	5

Grade: A

How to Earn a B Paper

A girl in the eighth grade wrote this report on volcanoes. It contains 760 words. Please read her paper below in its original form and then the discussion of her grade that follows.

Volcanoes

There have been many terrible volcanoes in this world, and seeing as volcanoes are what this report is about, I'll share a few with you now. This is not a complete list, it's just some of the majors.

At 8:30 am, May 18, 1980, Mount St. Helens in Washington erupted. Seismographic activity was recorded 20 miles north of Mount St. Helens by the University of Washington in Seattle on March 20th. This activity increased until March 27th, when she blew ash and vapor 20,000 feet into the air leaving a crater 250 feet in diameter. Two days later, on the 29th, another cloud of this sort reached as far south as Bend, Oregon, 150 miles south of Mount St. Helens. But, wait, I'm not done! After this, a bulge developed on the south side of the mountain that was 2,000 feet long and 500 feet high. Now, before I tell you what happened to this bulge, I have to say that this volcano was of a great help to expand our knowledge of volcanoes. Okay, back to this bulge. Well, it exploded on May 18, 1980, blowing ash 12 miles into the air. The impact knocked 150 square miles of trees down that were 20 miles away. When it blew, there was a landslide that displaced one river into another causing flooding. All and all, more than 100 people were dead or missing and there was $1.5 billion or more in total damage.

Another great volcano was in 79 A.D. when the mountain of Vesivius, Italy, destroyed Pompeii and Herculaneum. Ash rained down and it was as dark as night. Herculaneum was covered by mudflows while Pompeii was lost to ash and sulfur. The most interesting thing about Vesivius was that the townspeople got frozen in time. The ash and mud preserved the town perfectly. There were saloons with liquor stains on the counters and kitchens with pans and food still there. Almost everything was still intact.

April 5, 1815. It was thought to be extinct. Tambor, near Java, Indonesia, was 12,000 feet high. When it exploded, an unusual amount of ash went up into the atmosphere, changing the global climate. 1815 was called "the year with no summer." The winter wasn't bitter, but some inches of snow were reported in New England in June. Although, in New England there are many things that grow well and even thrive in the colder weather. This prompted Canada to buy some of our food, which, in turn, made grain prices soar. And in poor France political turmoil reigned, where they had just finished with the Napoleonic War. But back to the volcano. This large cloud darkened the sky for 300 miles away. The eruptions weren't over 'til July (at which

April 11-12 were the strongest). The site of the village of Tambora was covered with 18 feet of water and 12,000 natives died. In the end, the mountain of Tambora stood nearly one mile shorter than it was.

Arguably, this next one is the most well-known volcano in history. Krakatoa, Sunda Strait, Indonesia, August 26-27, 1883. Gases had built up inside Krakatoa. The island of Krakatoa destroyed itself. On the 27th explosions were heard from 5:30 am to 11:00 am from 3,000 miles away. Explosions that sent rocks flying into the air. The northern half of Krakatoa was completely gone and the explosions split Rakata from base to summit. This sent tsunamis that were reported to be 120 feet high ashore. Tens of thousands died from these tidal waves. The ash and vapor stayed in the atmosphere from the 1880's into the 1890's lowering the average temperature one degree Fahrenheit. These particles prompted a "green sun" in India. From the original island, Krakatoa, there's now Anak Krakatoa, Rakata, Pajanga and Sertung.

Another notable is Mount Pelee, Martinique. This explosion on May 8, 1902, wiped out the city of St. Pierre and killed more than 30,000 people with only six survivors, total. One of whom was a murderer named Joseph Surtout. He was locked away so far under that he was okay when they got him out four days later. This volcano was strange because there was no lava, only ashes, dust, gas and mud. Which was so thick, in fact, that when people called to each other, they could hear their own echoes.

As I said before, this list is far from complete. These volcanoes, along with many others, have impacted our lives heavily. But with every volcano eruption, comes more information about how to prepare and protect ourselves form future volcanoes.

CONTENT:

This student has done a lot of research on her subject, and she includes many interesting facts. This is commendable. She also puts the volcanoes into a logical order: most famous in recent history, then back to A.D. 79, 1815, 1883, and 1902 (in ascending order from history). Each volcano resides in its own paragraph. The student includes an introductory and a concluding paragraph. It is clear that she uses some organizational and note-taking skills.

She earned a B this way: Other than recounting famous volcanoes, her paper lacks a unifying theme. She mentions how studying volcanoes "was of a great help to expand our knowledge" of them, that volcanoes "have impacted our lives heavily," and that we now have "more information about how to prepare and protect ourselves from future volcanoes." Any of these would be excellent themes to develop in her paper, but she fails to expand on any of them.

Her introduction does not begin with an interesting story, statement, fact, quotation, or question. It also does not guide the reader into the body. Her conclusion includes some themes that are new to the paper, either of which would have been usable for the whole paper. The conclusion is not the place to introduce something new to the paper but should tie the end to the beginning, challenge the reader, or give the reader something to think about.

By the time a student reaches junior high, she should be able to choose a main idea and develop it throughout the paper. Her thesis statement should be clear and appear somewhere near the end of the first paragraph. In her head or in her notes, she should identify her main idea by stating, "In my paper, I want to say *this* about volcanoes." If she cannot identify her main idea in this way, she needs to back up and make some decisions about her topic, determining what she wants to say about it.

This student's tone (the attitude she brings to the subject) is too casual for a school paper. However, she has an easy writing style and usually tells a clear story. In paragraphs two and four, she moves off her stories but comes back to them quickly. If she had determined a unifying theme beforehand, she might not have gotten lost in those paragraphs.

GRAMMAR/MECHANICS:

On the whole, this is a fairly average eighth-grade paper. She usually uses commas correctly in dates and in places. There are a few other places that could have used some commas, especially to aid in clarity. She includes an apostrophe in her dates to indicate the decade, as in "1880's." It is now currently acceptable to write dates without the apostrophe, as in "1880s."

Instead of a comma in the last sentence of paragraph one, a semicolon should be used. It is one way of connecting two complete sentences.

Times of day use periods, as a.m. or p.m. Years are labeled as A.D. 79 or 35 B.C. The word *'til* should be written as *until* or *till.*

She misspells Vesuvius continually. In paragraph four, the reader has to guess whether the place name is Tambor or Tambora, as the writer uses both. Her third from the last word should be *from*, not *form*, something only careful reading will catch.

In paragraph four, she uses an acceptable sentence fragment: "But back to the volcano." However, in paragraphs five and six, she uses three unacceptable fragments: "Explosions that sent rocks flying into the air," "One of whom was a murderer named Joseph Surtout," and "Which was so thick, in fact, that when people called to each other, they could hear their own echoes."

In terms of the evaluation form for nonfiction, turn the page to see how this writer measures up.

CONTENT

	NO		Somewhat		YES
1. Did the student follow the assignment directions?	1	2	3	4	<u>5</u>
2. Does the paper begin with an interesting statement, fact, question, quote, or story?	<u>1</u>	2	3	4	5
3. Is the topic (subject matter) clear by reading the introductory paragraph?	1	2	3	4	<u>5</u>
4. Is there a clear thesis statement?	<u>1</u>	2	3	4	5
5. Is it near the end of the first paragraph? N/A	1	2	3	4	5
6. Does the paper support the thesis statement? N/A	1	2	3	4	5
7. Does the paper stick to the topic?	1	2	3	4	<u>5</u>
8. Are there transitions from one paragraph to the next?	1	2	<u>3</u>	4	5
9. Are there effective topic sentences?	1	2	3	<u>4</u>	5
10. Are the points clear and logical?	1	2	3	4	<u>5</u>
11. Are they in a logical order?	1	2	3	4	<u>5</u>
12. Does each point have good supporting statements?	1	2	3	4	<u>5</u>
13. Is the paper interesting or humorous?	1	2	3	4	<u>5</u>
14. Is it clear that the research was done well?	1	2	3	4	<u>5</u>
15. Does the paper show good use of the targeted writer's device (metaphor, transitions, etc.)? [a report]	1	2	<u>3</u>	4	5
16. Does the conclusion give food for thought, not just recount points?	1	2	<u>3</u>	4	5
17. Persuasion: Does the student follow the "Do List"?	1 N/A	2	3	4	5
18. Persuasion: Does the student avoid the "Don't List"?	1 N/A	2	3	4	5
19. Persuasion: Is there a call to action?	1 N/A	2	3	4	5

Grade: B

GRAMMAR/MECHANICS

	NO		Somewhat		YES	
1. Is there an introductory paragraph?	1	2	3	4	<u>5</u>	
2. Is there a separate paragraph for each point?	1	2	3	4	<u>5</u>	
3. Is there a concluding paragraph?	1	2	3	4	<u>5</u>	
4. Does the student avoid fragments except for effect?	1	2	<u>3</u>	4	5	
5. Does the student avoid run-on sentences?	1	2	3	4	<u>5</u>	
6. Does the student use good grammar?	1	2	3	4	<u>5</u>	
7. Does the student avoid jargon, lingo, or slang?	1	2	3	4	<u>5</u>	
8. If there is special jargon, is it defined? N/A	1	2	3	4	5	
9. Does the student use comma rules well?	1	2	<u>3</u>	4	5	
10. Is the rest of the punctuation/capitalization correct?	1	2	3	4	<u>5</u>	
11. Is the spelling correct?	1	2	3	<u>4</u>	5	Wasn't required
12. Are there varying sentence structures and lengths?	1	2	3	4	<u>5</u>	
13. Does the student correctly cite sources (reports, etc.)?	1	2	3	4	5 ←	
14. Is the paper double-spaced? [in the original]	<u>1</u>	2	3	4	5	

Grade: B

How to Earn a C Paper

Below is a persuasive paper written by a boy in the seventh grade. A persuasive paper aims at convincing the reader to think differently about a subject and to do something constructive in response (believe and behave a certain way).

Though he received a C on this paper, some of his other work is so good that it is included in the student workbook as an example of how to do something well.

Please read the following assignment, which is as he wrote it, and then read what this fellow did right and what he did wrong.

Conserve Natural Resources

I believe we need to conserve natural resources and I am going to state my opinion as well as other peoples opinions.

Many people do not believe it is necessary to conserve, because they mistakenly believe recources will last forever. Others know they need to conserve but do not care, because recources will not run out in their lifetime. The third group of people care and conserve resources.

Conservationists divide resources into four groups (1) inexhaustible resources such as sunlight and water (2) renewable resources like plants and animals (3) nonrenewable resources; most minerals fall into this category and (4) recycable resources some minerals and plastic go in this group.

There are many ways YOU can help save the environment. You can take newspapers and glass as well as plastic bottles to recycling centers. You can stop forests and jungles from being cut down, and many other ways.

Conservation is important to maintain the quality of life wich means to keep the environment healthy.

CONTENT:

This young writer does a few things well. His title is clear and to the point. He mentions that some people do not take conservation seriously—a view opposite to his. He educates the reader about the categories of natural resources, which indicates some level of research. He also suggests a few things the reader can do to help the environment. His last sentence contains what might be his thesis statement (main idea). He has an introductory paragraph, three paragraphs for a body, and a concluding paragraph—a good format to use.

The obvious question that comes to mind is this: Did he use an outline? It is unlikely that he did. While he talks about the issue from many angles, he does not focus on one area or lead the reader from point to point in any logical progression. He mentions an opposing view but does not refute it. He does not develop the idea of four kinds of natural resources and what the reader can do about each one. In listing ways the reader could respond, he omits how the reader can "stop forests and jungles from being cut down."

His introduction does not begin with an interesting statement, fact, question, quotation, or story. He uses "I believe…" (see the Don't List, page 50).The introduction states what he is going to tell the reader instead of engaging the reader in the topic. The thesis statement belongs at the end of his first paragraph, not at the end of his paper.

His conclusion should use something that refers to his clever statement, fact, question, quotation, or story (which he omitted) in the introduction, and it should contain a call to action (which was in his fourth paragraph).

His persuasive paper reads more like a simple report on conservation.

Because this paper was this student's first try at persuasion, it was important to encourage him instead of list all his deficiencies. Comments included what he did well and how his paper could be stronger (use an outline, focus on one element of conservation, refute opposite view points, and so forth).   There's no sense in shooting down the bird you're trying to teach how to fly.

GRAMMAR/MECHANICS:

Words directly related to the topic should be spelled correctly. *Resources* is misspelled twice, *recyclable* once.

Peoples (paragraph one) should be *people's. Wich* (paragraph five) should be *which.*

This writer does a brave thing in his list in paragraph three. He uses a numerical method of listing, even though he does not punctuate it correctly. This is one correct way of fixing it:

Conservationists divide resources into four groups: (1) inexhaustible resources such as sunlight and water; (2) renewable resources like plants and animals; (3) nonrenewable resources—most minerals fall into this category; and (4) recyclable resources, including plastic and some minerals.

The word *because* normally does not get a comma before it; it is not a coordinating conjunction (*but, and, for, or, nor, yet,* and *so*) but a lowly subordinating conjunction. This is a common mistake.

The first sentence in his paper is a compound sentence and deserves a comma before the word *and*.   This paper is a solid C grade in content and a B- in grammar/mechanics.

In terms of the evaluation form for nonfiction, here is how this student measures up:

CONTENT

	NO		Somewhat		YES
1. Did the student follow the assignment directions?	1	2	**3**	4	5
2. Does the paper begin with an interesting statement, fact, question, quote, or story?	**1**	2	3	4	5
3. Is the topic (subject matter) clear by reading the introductory paragraph?	1	2	3	4	**5**
4. Is there a clear thesis statement?	1	**2**	3	4	5
5. Is it near the end of the first paragraph?	1	2	3	**4**	5
6. Does the paper support the thesis statement?	1	**2**	3	4	5
7. Does the paper stick to the topic?	1	2	3	**4**	5
8. Are there transitions from one paragraph to the next?	**1**	2	3	4	5
9. Are there effective topic sentences?	1	2	**3**	4	5
10. Are the points clear and logical?	1	2	**3**	4	5
11. Are they in a logical order?	1	2	**3**	4	5
12. Does each point have good supporting statements?	**1**	2	3	4	5
13. Is it interesting or humorous?	1	2	**3**	4	5
14. Is it clear that the research was done well?	1	2	**3**	4	5
15. Does the paper show good use of the targeted writer's device (metaphor, transitions, etc.)? [persuasion]	**1**	2	3	4	5
16. Does the conclusion give food for thought, not just recount points?	1	2	3	**4**	5
17. Persuasion: Does the student follow the "Do List"?	1	2	**3**	4	5
18. Persuasion: Does the student avoid the "Don't List"?	1	2	**3**	4	5
19. Persuasion: Is there a call to action?	1	2	**3**	4	5

Grade: C

GRAMMAR/MECHANICS

	NO		Somewhat		YES
1. Is there an introductory paragraph?	1	2	3	4	**5**
2. Is there a separate paragraph for each point?	1	2	3	4	**5**
3. Is there a concluding paragraph?	1	2	3	4	**5**
4. Does the student avoid fragments except for effect?	1	2	3	4	**5**
5. Does the student avoid run-on sentences?	1	2	3	4	**5**
6. Does the student use good grammar?	1	2	3	4	**5**
7. Does the student avoid jargon, lingo, or slang?	1	2	3	4	**5**
8. If there is special jargon, is it defined? N/A	1	2	3	4	5
9. Does the student use comma rules well?	1	2	**3**	4	5
10. Is the rest of the punctuation/capitalization correct?	1	2	3	**4**	5
11. Is the spelling correct?	1	2	**3**	4	5
12. Are there varying sentence structures and lengths?	1	2	**3**	4	5
13. Does the student correctly cite sources (reports, etc.)?	1	N/A 2	**3**	4	5
14. Is the paper double-spaced?	**1**	2	3	4	5

Grade: B –

How to Earn a D Paper

It is interesting to note that students who do well with one type of writing might do poorly with another. The following paper is a perfect example of this enigma. This boy in the seventh grade did so well with another type of writing that he is featured in the student workbook as an example of how to do something right.

Please read the following persuasive assignment. Then read what this fellow did right and what he did wrong. The word minimum was 300; he wrote 359. The paper appears as he wrote it, except that his copy was double-spaced.

What Are Things Coming To?

What are things coming to nowadays? I mean, you can't hardly even get a new system with FIFTEEN morally good games. By systems and games I mean video games, the makers are going money crazy. Can't they make enough money by making more E (Everyone) rated games because if they have to make games as bad as some of the ones they do just to survive (which I'm sure they don't) then I would say, "Go work at McDonalds!"

If I were to take 50 randomly selected X-Box games probably only 10-15 (and that's if you're lucky) would be E-rated, *every other one* would be either T (Teen) rated or M (Mature), that's just pitiful! Also, I agree with parents who think that some videogames can make kids more violent.

Imagine this: you get home from school, do your homework, and maybe even fix yourself a little snack, but then you go up to your room and play videogames for a few hours, where all you try to do is kill as many people as you can and get excited when you get a better weapon so you can kill more people. Do you think that some of that might rub off on you? Think long and hard on that one, duh, of course it will, at least a little. And that might, just might have something to do with all the school shootings from teens that are going on. Plus you can never possibly keep up with all the systems & games that keep coming out.

My point on that is because you buy a PlayStation, out comes a PS2, a Nintendo 64, out comes a Gamecube, a PS2, out comes a PS3, I mean it's honestly pathetic. My cousin for example (not to make him look bad, he doesn't have any bad games or anything), keeps getting new stuff. Like he had a PS and a lot of games, then he wanted a PS2. So he traded in his PS and *10 games*, originally worth at least $250 to $300, so he only had to pay 20 dollars for a PS2, which should've only cost $200! And that's supposed to be a good deal! On the other hand though, there are a lot of people kinda like my cousin who don't have any bad games, but there are so many bad games, and they look so cool that some people who don't want to may end up buying 1 or 2 of them. And as a Christian I believe that we shouldn't let ourselves fall for the temptation of the bad games. I hope that you will help make this world come to better things, by not playing or buying any evil games, even if your friends do.

CONTENT:

This young writer does a few things right. He defines the ratings on the games just after he mentions them. He also links video game violence to real-world violence, something that researchers have successfully done. Transition sentences appear at the end of paragraphs two and three. He includes a call to action in the last sentence. It is clear that he feels strongly about his subject.

However, his writing is like an out-of-control trapeze artist—swinging from one idea to the next—and he is working without a net, which is an outline or at least a list of points in a logical order. It is obvious that he did not list any points before he began writing or arrange any points for a good flow of ideas. Although the reader knows in the first paragraph how the writer feels about the topic, there is no thesis statement on which the reader can focus his attention. This shows that the writer did not write a purpose statement to guide his writing ("I will convince the reader that…").

Such phrases as "the makers are going money crazy," "that's just pitiful!" "duh," "it's honestly pathetic," and so forth, show that the writer is simply yelling at his audience. Ranting and raving is definitely on the Don't List of persuasive writing and should be avoided. Yelling at the reader instead of instructing or leading him automatically lowers the grade.

His one valid point about violence is weakened by the fact that he did not do any research or cite any authorities on the subject. This would have strengthened his argument and made it sound more valid.

Telling a story usually gives a point some muscle, but his scenario and his story only water down what he had hoped to say.

His concluding paragraph is not separate but added to the fourth paragraph.

What is his paper about? Greedy game makers? The abundance of T- and M-rated games? The violence spawned by playing these games? The proliferation of new game systems and their cost? That Christians shouldn't succumb to the temptation to play violent games? It's hard to tell.

To earn a higher grade, this normally good writer should have narrowed his focus, written a purpose statement for his own benefit, listed his points and ordered them before writing, included a thesis statement in the first paragraph, used his paragraphs to support his points, included research and/or quotations from experts, and finished with a strong call to action—all without yelling at his reader. Writing with a positive, we-can-fix-this attitude is always more effective than using a negative, in-your-face tone.

Summing up, he needs organization, focus, a thesis statement, good format (introductory paragraph, one paragraph for each point in the body, and a concluding paragraph), something in the first paragraph to engage the reader in the topic, facts from research, a clear call to action, and a positive tone.

GRAMMAR/MECHANICS:

This student correctly defines game ratings and capitalizes the names of the game systems.

He uses a double negative in the second sentence. There are many run-on sentences. By using parentheses to add asides, he breaks the flow of his writing. He should use parentheses sparingly and only when needed, as when he defines the video game ratings. Instead of an ampersand (&), he should use the word *and* in paragraph three. A review of comma rules would be helpful. This is a solid D paper in content and C in grammar/mechanics.

In terms of the evaluation form for nonfiction, here is how this student measures up:

CONTENT

	NO		Somewhat		YES
1. Did the student follow the assignment directions?	1	2	**3**	4	5
2. Does the paper begin with an interesting statement, fact, question, quote, or story?	**1**	2	3	4	5
3. Is the topic (subject matter) clear by reading the introductory paragraph?	1	2	3	**4**	5
4. Is there a clear thesis statement?	**1**	2	3	4	5
5. Is it near the end of the first paragraph? N/A	1	2	3	4	5
6. Does the paper support the thesis statement? N/A	1	2	3	4	5
7. Does the paper stick to the topic?	1	2	**3**	4	5
8. Are there transitions from one paragraph to the next?	1	2	3	**4**	5
9. Are there effective topic sentences?	**1**	2	3	4	5
10. Are the points clear and logical?	1	**2**	3	4	5
11. Are they in a logical order?	**1**	2	3	4	5
12. Does each point have good supporting statements?	**1**	2	3	4	5
13. Is the paper interesting or humorous?	**1**	2	3	4	5
14. Is it clear that the research was done well?	**1**	2	3	4	5
15. Does the paper show good use of the targeted writer's device (metaphor, transitions, etc.)? [persuasion]	**1**	2	3	4	5
16. Does the conclusion give food for thought, not just recount points?	1	2	3	**4**	5
17. Persuasion: Does the student follow the "Do List"?	1	**2**	3	4	5
18. Persuasion: Does the student avoid the "Don't List"?	1	**2**	3	4	5
19. Persuasion: Is there a call to action?	1	2	**3**	4	5

Grade: D

GRAMMAR/MECHANICS

	NO		Somewhat		YES
1. Is there an introductory paragraph?	1	2	3	4	**5**
2. Is there a separate paragraph for each point?	1	2	**3**	4	5
3. Is there a concluding paragraph?	**1**	2	3	4	5
4. Does the student avoid fragments except for effect?	1	2	3	**4**	5
5. Does the student avoid run-on sentences?	**1**	2	3	4	5
6. Does the student use good grammar?	1	2	**3**	4	5
7. Does the student avoid jargon, lingo, or slang?	1	2	3	4	**5**
8. If there is special jargon, is it defined?	1	2	3	4	**5**
9. Does the student use comma rules well?	1	**2**	3	4	5
10. Is the rest of the punctuation/capitalization correct?	1	2	3	**4**	5
11. Is the spelling correct?	1	2	3	4	**5**
12. Are there varying sentence structures and lengths?	1	2	**3**	4	5
13. Does the student correctly cite sources (reports, etc.)? 1 N/A	2	3	4	5	
14. Is the paper double-spaced? [Yes, in the original.] 1	2	3	4	**5**	

Grade: C

How to Earn an F Paper

Few are the things a student can do to earn an F on a paper. Below is a list of things that, to this writer's mind, deserve an F. Perhaps you can think of some to add to the list.

- Not doing the assignment
- Not following the directions for the assignment (other than a simple misunderstanding)
- Handing in the assignment very late (Consider subtracting one grade for each day the assignment is late. If the paper is one day late and deserves an A-, give a B+ or a B instead.)
- Plagiarizing

10-Minute Writing Plunges Program
- Guidelines -

- There are enough **Writing Plunges** to last all year.

- These are designed to encourage reluctant writers and delight eager ones. Think of the words *fun* and *interesting*.

- Give a new prompt to your student every Monday, Tuesday, Wednesday, and Thursday. Your student will write for 10 minutes, keep his own work, and not be graded on it—yet.

- On Friday your student will choose which paper he likes best, then he will proofread it and get it ready to hand in on the following Monday for a grade.

- Avoid using the **Writing Plunges** while your student is working in the workbook portion of this book unless you want to spark creativity and forgo the grades.

- **Writing Plunges** can be a fun break from the workbook or can be used as a yearlong program by itself.

- Students in classroom settings may want to volunteer to read their work aloud.

- Substitute a Grab Bag for a prompt once a month. Put something fun in the bag and have your student write about it (a cookie, an interesting picture, an unusual object, etc.).

- Feel free to substitute your own writing prompts.

10-Minute Writing Plunges for September

Week One

1. You have just created a new dessert. Name it and write a short description of it for the menu.
2. "I just can't stand…"
3. "I'll never go there again!" (what happened and why you won't go back)
4. Kryptonite made Superman weak. What is your kryptonite?

Week Two

1. "I think the president should…"
2. What book can't you stand? Explain why you won't ever read it again.
3. "The most ugly thing I ever saw was…"
4. Write about your best friend. Use the hand you normally don't write with.

Week Three

1. "If I could cure any disease…"
2. "God has given me…"
3. Write about a food you just can't get enough of.
4. Write about a favorite autumn memory.

Week Four

1. "Something good about me is…"
2. "Something bad about me is…"
3. Write a prayer.
4. Write about the perfect day. Choose the form in which you want to write about it: poem, essay, short story, pretend journal entry, and so forth.

10-Minute Writing Plunges for October

Week One

1. "A smart thing I once did was…"
2. Write about a smell you can't stand.
3. Find a very exciting part in a book. Write it out in your notebook or on the computer. Figure out what makes it exciting.
4. What do you like to do when you are alone?

Week Two

1. Pretend that your house is for sale. Write a real-estate ad. (Look in the newspaper for examples or get real-estate ads free at stores.)
2. What time period would you like to visit? Explain.
3. Write a humorous story about a stupid or embarrassing thing you once did.
4. "A habit I'd like to break is…"

Week Three

1. What do you wish you had done on your last vacation or day off?
2. Write a fictional story using a famous person from history.
3. What advice would you like to give someone?
4. Imagine you are a parent. Try to convince your child to do a particular chore.

Week Four

1. Draw the floor plan of your house. Put another family in it and describe one of their meals together. Write their conversation.
2. Write a police description of a criminal.
3. What superpower do you wish you had? How would you use it?
4. Write the last paragraph of your autobiography.

10-Minute Writing Plunges for November

Week One

1. You've just had an accident. What kind of accident was it? Describe what happened.
2. Write about a special talent or trait you have.
3. You are writing a children's book titled *Come Back*. Write the first paragraph.
4. What is the opposite of love? Explain.

Week Two

1. Write a prayer of thanks to God.
2. "If I had been a pilgrim, I would have…"
3. Invent a new children's cereal. Name it and write a TV commercial for it.
4. Describe a real or pretend walk in the woods.

Week Three

1. You have an opportunity to go overseas. Which country will you choose? What will you do there?
2. Write a greeting card for Thanksgiving. Decorate it if you wish.
3. Write a speech about freedom.
4. Pretend you are Mother Goose. Make up a nursery rhyme.

Week Four

1. Describe yourself to a new pen pal.
2. What can you do with a tree?
3. Write a letter to a friend (real or pretend) who is discouraged.
4. You found bad news when you researched your family tree. What did you find? Who will you tell and how?

10-Minute Writing Plunges for December

Week One

1. Find a very dull part in a book. Figure out why it is so dull. Are the characters wishy-washy? Is the plot uninteresting and slow? Is the conflict (problem) too small? Is the description too long? Rewrite it and make it interesting.
2. "My favorite thing to talk about is…"
3. Write the first paragraph of a story that happens on Mars.
4. You just gave someone a gift, but he or she doesn't like it. Write the conversation.

Week Two

1. Write a paragraph about Christmas using words of only one syllable.
2. On the left side of your paper, write everyone's name in your family. Next to each name, write one thing about him or her that you like or admire.
3. You received a present from an aunt. You like the aunt, but the present is horrible. Write a polite thank-you letter to your aunt for the present.
4. Write about a time you were brave (or wished you had been).

10-Minute Writing Plunges for January

Week One

1. What is your favorite food? Describe its taste, smell, and texture.
2. What do you like to do to make someone happy?
3. Close your eyes or put a bandanna over them for 5 minutes. Pretend you are blind. What do you hear? Write your impressions.
4. What is the worst thing someone can say to someone else?

Week Two

1. If you weren't in school today, what would you be doing?
2. Write a prayer for someone.
3. You are going on a trip, but you can only take five things with you. What will you take and why? (No fair listing a full backpack or a bulging piece of luggage as one of your five items!)
4. The most important of the Ten Commandments is _____ because…

Week Three

1. If you could spend a day with a famous person, living or dead (not deity), who would it be and what would you do?
2. Write a poem about your favorite color.
3. Pretend that everyone is out of the house for four hours. What are you going to do?
4. Design a new coin. Write a letter to the U. S. mint and tell them why they should use your coin and design.

Week Four

1. "If I could teach someone something…"
2. Write a list of everything you believe about God.
3. Skip a meal (if you are medically able to) and write what it feels like.
4. Write a story concerning an article of clothing.

10-Minute Writing Plunges for February

Week One

1. "I was very embarrassed when…"
2. "Once I dreamt…"
3. "My pet peeves are…"
4. Write out your favorite Bible verse and explain why you like it.

Week Two

1. Write an ad for something you want to sell. Make it sound wonderful!
2. Write a new script for your favorite TV show or for a new TV show.
3. You are locked out of your house. What will you do?
4. Write the story of "Jack and the Beanstalk" as a sports report.

Week Three

1. "I can't wait to be older so I can…"
2. "The easiest thing in the world for me to do is…"
3. An odor can make you remember something you'd forgotten. Write about the last time you remembered something because of a smell.
4. "Someone once told me…"

Week Four

1. "If I could give someone anything that belongs to me…"
2. Pick up an item and close your eyes. Feel the item for a few minutes and then write how it felt—its textures, temperature, different surfaces, etc.
3. Write the journal entry of a teacher on a particularly difficult day.
4. "I would like to read or learn about…"

10-Minute Writing Plunges for March

Week One

1. Write your opinion of a sports figure of your choice.
2. What instrument in a band or orchestra would you like to be?
3. There is too much _____ in the world today. Explain.
4. What item from your childhood do you treasure? Write a short story using it as the main character.

Week Two

1. Invent a warning that will go on a sign or a product. Draw a picture if necessary.
2. Write about a collection you have or would like to begin.
3. "When I am 25, I am going to…"
4. Change the ending of a familiar movie. Make the characters do something else.

Week Three

1. "If I could redecorate my room…"
2. Choose a game. Write the instructions for how to play it.
3. Write the story of Snow White from a dwarf's point of view.
4. Write a poem about your favorite season.

Week Four

1. "God's favorite color must be _____ because…"
2. You are a famous meteorologist. Invent and write tomorrow's weather forecast.
3. If you could have three wishes, what would they be?
4. "What I fear most is…"

10-Minute Writing Plunges for April

Week One

1. "The next time I get the chance, I'm going to…"
2. "The best part about my last trip was…"
3. Design a new traffic sign. Draw the shape of the sign and what goes on it. Write a TV commercial to explain to the public what it means.
4. Write a Sunday school lesson.

Week Two

1. A superhero enters your room. What happens next?
2. What makes your heart pound?
3. Write a conversation between two people who have just had a car accident with each other.
4. "I'm too old to…"

Week Three

1. Read Jesus' parable of the prodigal son. Which character do you identify with in the story? Explain.
2. "The things I love to hear are…"
3. Invent an older brother or sister. Describe him or her and tell what you would do together for one day.
4. Write a story using all the words from your spelling list.

Week Four

1. "I would regret it if I never…"
2. A friend has asked you for advice. What is the problem, and what advice will you give?
3. Which sport would you compete in if you were in the Winter or Summer Olympics?
4. "I wish…"

10-Minute Writing Plunges for May

Week One

1. You are painting a picture. What is it? Where are you?
2. Create a new holiday. How will people celebrate it?
3. Write a letter to a fictional character you admire or can't stand.
4. Something you just bought isn't right. Write a letter to the store or manufacturer.

Week Two

1. You just won a shopping spree at a store. Which store? What will you buy?
2. "I often dream (or daydream) about…"
3. Write a sermon.
4. You need a summer job. Describe yourself to an employer.

Week Three

1. You hear your pet talking. What is he/she saying?
2. Pretend you have a scar. How did you get it?
3. "I often pray about/for…"
4. List five words at random from any book. Write a story that includes all five.

Week Four

1. Write a blurb (the stuff on the back cover) for your favorite book.
2. Write a story about a person who just bought squid for supper.
3. Describe the feeling of falling.
4. Think of the person you like the most and the person you like the least. Write a conversation between them.

DON'T List

(Students have this list in "Persuasion: The Basics," Skill 9, pages 44 and 45.)

1. **Don't insult** or single out a person or an entire group.
Wrong: Did you kids even look at yourselves in the mirror before you left the house? You're a mess!

2. **Don't wander** off your subject.
Wrong: I hope the library buys *Out of the Dust* by Karen Hesse. I read a lot of books. Just last week I read four books from the Left Behind series and two by Frank Peretti. Those men sure are good writers. I want to read more by them.

3. **Don't contradict** yourself.
Wrong: The team sure could use me at first base. That's my favorite position unless I'm playing shortstop.

4. **Don't go on and on.** Keep it short and sweet.
Wrong: Putting a statue in the middle of our park was so stupid. I mean, who needs another statue? We already have four around town. Why do we need one more bronze hero up on a horse? Our town will get a bad reputation for all the statues we have, and no one knows who those guys are anymore.

5. **Don't use "I think…,"** "I believe…," or "It is my opinion that…."
Wrong: It is my opinion that abortion is wrong. **Right:** Abortion is wrong.

6. **Don't write without evidence;** don't exclude facts.
Wrong: Probably some other towns have recycling bins too. I can't think of any right now, but I'm sure there are some.

7. **Don't be vague.**
Wrong: I want to talk to you about a problem in our town. It has been here for a long time. Everyone is bothered by it. Can't you see how bad it has gotten in the past year? Isn't it awful? And now it's time to do something about it.

8. **Don't be illogical;** don't draw the wrong conclusions.
Wrong: No one waited on me, even though I was there first. I know it was because of my red hair and freckles. The employees must hate red hair and freckles. They waited on two blondes before they would even look at me.

9. **Don't use jargon** (lingo) or technical words that only a few know.
Wrong: Be sure to attach the widget to the doohickey just under the spanner.

10. **Don't threaten** your audience or rant and rave.
Wrong: If I were you, I would watch out from now on! The next time I go into your red-hair-and-freckles-hating store, I'm going to do some damage! You'll see. You can't ignore me and get away with it.

DO List

(Students have this list in "Persuasion: The Basics," Skill 9, pages 45 and 46.)

1. **Do treat** your reader intelligently.
Right: Teens, please show that you respect yourselves by dressing modestly.

2. **Do talk fairly** about the opposing view.
Right: Many women say that abortion is an important part of women's rights. They want to be able to make decisions for themselves about their bodies. And that seems logical until you realize that there are a lot of little girls who will never have any rights because someone made the decision of death for them.

3. **Do quote** people, experts, or the Bible.
Right: I'm the right person for the first base position. Even Coach McGraw said last year, "If you want first base done right, rely on Pat. Nobody's better."

4. **Do be clear** about your topic.
Right: When I finished reading *Out of the Dust*, I knew other teens would like it. That's why I hope the library buys it.

5. **Do identify yourself** if it adds to your topic.
Right: I don't want the new highway to go through Vine Street. I should know. I've lived there all my life. **Right:** I am a frequent babysitter, so I know the importance of first aid training.

6. **Do define** your terms.
Right: Open your bumbershoot (umbrella) with care.

7. **Do know your audience.** Know their age, gender, interests, and so forth.
Wrong for a newspaper: Various personages subscribe to the fortuitous vicissitudes of existence. (This means that some people believe in chance, but it is too wordy for a newspaper, which is normally written for a 12-year-old reading level.)

Wrong: If you write a letter to the editor of your city's newspaper about how your church should have blue hymnals instead of red, you will be forgetting that most of the readers don't attend your church.

Right: When you write that article on friendship for *Brio* magazine (published by Focus on the Family), you will write it for Christian girls who are 12 to 16 years old.

Right: When you give your Christian testimony in church, you will use words and phrases that everyone there understands. But when you give your testimony to a friend who is not a Christian and who hasn't ever been to church, you will use words that he understands. You will mean the same thing, but you will use different words.

Different Ways to Write Biographies
(Students have this list in Exposition: A Biography, Skill 2, page 102.)

1. Write about a person's accomplishments: If he hadn't been born, then we wouldn't have _____ (or we wouldn't know _____).

2. Write about the part of his childhood that is the key to his future accomplishments.

3. Write about someone you respect. Use his accomplishments and difficulties to show why you respect him.

4. Write about someone you don't respect. Don't choose a family member or neighbor! Choose a person from history or a person in the public eye today. Write about his negative accomplishments or his character flaws to show why you don't respect him.

5. Write a "Who Am I?" in which you tell interesting things about the person but save the name for near the end of your biography.

6. Write about an important or pivotal day in the life of your person. Show what happened and how it changed him.

7. Write about a person's spiritual development throughout his life.

8. Write an imaginary page from your person's journal, diary, or letter. Show the reader what your person was like. Include facts.

A Book Response

(Students have this list in "A Book Response," Skill 1, pages 129 and 130.)

ARTISTIC SKILLS

1. **Draw, paint, or sculpt** an interesting character or scene from the book. Label the work or include a caption.

2. **Create a mural** with friends. Illustrate a setting or a scene.

3. Make a **3-D scene** in a box (a diorama) to illustrate a section of the story. Use the author's description of that scene. Try to capture the mood too.

4. **Draw a map** for the inside cover of the book, labeling the lands that people in the story traveled in. If it is a journey, show the beginning and the destination. Don't forget the dangerous places. Color your map if you want to.

5. Research the kinds of clothes (or weapons, houses, cars, furniture, etc.) the people in your story might have used. **Draw or paint** pictures of them, **build** a model or replica, or **sew** the clothes.

6. **Act out** an important scene from the book with a friend or two in front of an audience. Use costumes and props.

WRITING SKILLS

7. Make a **report card** for the author. Grade him on the basics: setting, characters, plot, etc. Also grade him on how he began and ended the book, if the book held your attention, if he used similes and metaphors, etc. Include why you gave him those grades and what he can do to improve.

8. Write a **story or poem** of your own based on something you read in the book.

9. Write a **letter to the author.** Ask something about the book or mention what you learned from it. If the author is still living, you can send your letter to the publisher listed on the inside of your book.

10. Write a letter to an **imaginary librarian** telling her why she should buy this book for the library. Include a little bit about the book, why it will appeal to other readers, and why you liked it.

11. Write a **blurb** (the part of the story you find on the back cover of the book). Tell enough of the story to get the reader interested—but don't tell the ending!

12. Write a **negative blurb** as on the backs of A Series of Unfortunate Events books, telling the reader why he should *not* read the book. This is using reverse psychology. The more you tell the reader not to read it, the more he will want to.

13. Write a pretend **telephone conversation** between you and a friend. Tell her why you think she would like the story and what you liked about it. Or warn her about it and say what you *didn't* like.

14. Read about any **animals** in the book and write a short report or give a short speech on them.

15. Write a **television commercial** for the book. Include what you liked about it. Then read it to an interested audience.

Grammar Resources

Christian Book Distributors

1-800-CHRISTIAN (1-800-247-4784)
www.christianbook.com

CBD's Homeschool Catalog showcases many practical grammar books and guides.

CliffsQuickReview™ *Writing: Grammar, Usage, and Style*

Published by Wiley Publishing
10475 Crosspoint Blvd.
Indianapolis, IN 46256
1-800-762-2974

Also available at www.cliffsnotes.com, this book is a handy reference guide for both grammar and writing. It is designed for high school students.

Easy Grammar Series by Wanda C. Phillips

ISHA Enterprises
P.O. Box 25970
Scottsdale, AZ 85255
1-800-641-6015
www.easygrammar.com

You can trust the title of this series! I highly recommend these books, especially for young or reluctant grammar students. Each *Easy Grammar* workbook, in addition to being student-friendly, contains an easy reference guide to grammar facts. The short and easy *Daily Grams* are engineered to review and reinforce facts already learned.

Editor in Chief Series from Critical Thinking Books and Software

P.O. Box 1610
Seaside, CA 93955
1-800-458-4849
www.CriticalThinking.com

These workbooks review and reinforce grammar facts that the student has already learned. The student searches for mistakes in short articles and picture captions. The workbooks contain an easy reference guide to grammar facts.

Scholastic.com

This is an excellent site for students and parents. Scholastic has all sorts of useful books on grammar, vocabulary, writing, and so forth.

Writing Strands: Evaluating Writing from National Writing Institute

Writing Strands
624 W. University Drive, Suite 248
Denton, TX 76201
1-800-688-5375
www.writingstrands.com

This is a helpful book for those who would like more information on how to evaluate their students' composition papers. The author, David Marks, has included examples of students' work from many age levels and has made this book very practical.

Your local bookstore

These folks always stock grammar guides and reference books for students at the beginning of each school year. Take advantage of a full array of products during those months.

Answer Key

Answer Key

➡ **Getting Your Feet Wet**, Skill 1, pp. 5,6: *Answers will vary.*

⇨ **Getting Your Feet Wet**, Skill 2, pp. 8,10: *Answers will vary.*

⇨ **Getting Your Feet Wet**, Skill 3, pp. 11,12: *Answers will vary.*

➡ **Opinions—You've Got Them**, Skill 1, pp. 13,14: *Answers will vary.*

⇨ **Opinions**, Skill 2, pp. 15,16:

1. *He has shown talent by breaking a league record.*
2. *He feels he was born to play soccer.*
3. *His parents and coach are all supporting him.*

⇨ **Opinions**, Skill 3, pp. 17,18: *Answers will vary.*

⇨ **Opinions**, Skill 4, p. 20:

List the two things the writer used to prove that cats are clean.
    1. *They constantly lick themselves clean.*
    2. *They can be trained to use a kitty litter box.*

⇨ **Opinions**, Skill 5, p. 22: *Answers will vary.*

⇨ **Opinions**, Skill 6, p. 24: *Answers will vary.*

⇨ **Opinions**, Skill 7, p. 26:

1. Does she have an interesting first sentence? *Personal opinion, hopefully "yes."*
2. How did she tie her conclusion to her introduction? *She called the cello her peg-legged friend again.*
3. In paragraphs four and five, what are her reasons for liking the cello? *Paragraph four: the teacher. Paragraph five: She likes to perform.*
4. After reading this, do you think you would like to play the cello? *Personal opinion*

➡ **Persuasion: The Basics**, Skill 1, p. 30: *Answers will vary.*

⇨ **Persuasion: The Basics**, Skill 2, pp. 31,32: *Answers will vary.*

⇨ **Persuasion: The Basics**, Skill 3, p. 33: *Answers will vary.*

⇨ **Persuasion: The Basics**, Skill 4, p. 35: *Answers will vary.*

⇨ **Persuasion: The Basics**, Skill 5, p. 37: *Answers will vary.*

⇨ **Persuasion: The Basics**, Skill 6, pp. 38,39: *Answers will vary.*

⇨ **Persuasion: The Basics**, Skill 7, pp. 40,41:

1. Did his first sentence make you want to read more? *Personal opinion, hopefully "yes."*
2. List the five reasons why he liked *Spider-Man*. *1) lots of action, 2) exciting movie, 3) suspense, 4) explains where he got his powers, 5) strong villain*
3. If you have seen the movie, do you agree with his reasons? *Personal opinion*
4. If you have not see the movie, do his reasons make you want to see it? *Personal opinion*
5. Have you heard anything negative about this movie? If so, what are the negative things this boy didn't include? *Answers will vary.*
6. Write the purpose statement this writer might have used. *I am going to convince the reader that* Spider-Man *is a good movie to watch.*
7. What was his call to action? *Watch or rewatch the movie.*
8. Based on what you now know about persuasive writing, what grade would you give this writer? *Personal opinion*

⇨ **Persuasion: The Basics**, Skill 8, pp. 42,43: *Answers will vary.*

⇨ **Persuasion: The Basics**, Skill 9, p. 46: *Answers will vary.*

➔ **Cause and Effect**, Skill 1, p. 50: *Answers will vary.*

⇨ **Cause and Effect**, Skill 2, pp. 51, 53: *Answers will vary.*

⇨ **Cause and Effect**, Skill 3, p. 55: *Answers will vary.*

⇨ **Cause and Effect**, Skill 4, pp. 56,57: *Answers will vary.*

⇨ **Cause and Effect**, Skill 5, pp. 58,59:

1. Did the first sentence interest you? *Personal opinion*
2. How did the writer let you know the refrigerator is a good invention without saying, "The refrigerator is good"? *By writing "ice-cold sodas," "fresh garden vegetables," "handy refrigerators," and "wonderful ways it would be used".*
3. Why was the last sentence a good one to end with? *It was clever, and it tied in with the first sentence.*

4. What were the writer's three reasons why the refrigerator is good? *1) helps the medical profession, 2) healthier lifestyles, 3) makes flowers and floral arrangements more available*

5. What order did the writer use for the reasons? (one of the importance orders, chronological order, or effect-size order) *Importance: most, next, least*

6. Based on your knowledge of cause and effect, what grade would you give this student? *Answers will vary*

➜ **Exposition: The Basics**, Skill 1, pp. 64,65: *Answers will vary.*

⇨ **Exposition: The Basics**, Skill 2, pp. 66,67: *Reconstructed paragraph:*

The calendar that we use today hasn't always been around. At first, people kept track of the year by the seasons. They knew that things began to grow again at the same time every year. Today we call that season *spring*. Later, people paid attention to the moon and its phases (new moon, full moon, etc.). The phases were named for the different shapes the moon seems to have. The time it takes for the moon to go through all its phases is about 29 ½ days. That time became known as a *month*, named for the moon.

⇨ **Exposition: The Basics**, Skill 3, pp. 69,70: *Answers will vary.*

⇨ **Exposition: The Basics**, Skill 4, p. 72: *Answers will vary.*

⇨ **Exposition: The Basics**, Skill 5, p. 73: *Answers will vary. Here is one possible paraphrase:*

It's been eighty-seven years since we first began our nation and wrote the famous idea into the Constitution that everyone is equal.

This Civil War we're in is a test to see if we can stay together as a nation. These brave men fought and died here so that we could stay a nation. We're going to create a new cemetery and bury them here. It's the right thing to do.

⇨ **Exposition: The Basics**, Skill 6, p. 77:

Taylor, Paul S. The Great Dinosaur Mystery and the Bible. San Diego: Master Books, 1987.

Humber, Paul. "The Ascent of Racism." Impact, Feb. 1987. http://www.icr.org/pubs/imp/imp-164.htm (accessed June 14, 2005).

⇨ **Exposition: The Basics**, Skill 7, p.79,80:

Food
Panamanian staples: rice, corn, legumes and beans, yams, cassava (an edible root), plantains (a kind of banana)
sancocho—rich, hearty soup made with chicken and vegetables
tamales—of cornmeal dough, stuffed with chicken, pork, or vegetables, wrapped in banana leaves and boiled
arroz con guando—rice and beans cooked in coconut milk
hojaldras—flat dough fried, sometimes with sprinkled sugar
lots of seafood

People
a "melting pot" of ethnic cultures
more than 3 million people
Native Americans
Kuna Indians in the San Blas Islands
descendants of black slaves (brought to dive for pearls years ago)
descendants of Spanish from the 1500s to the 1800s
descendants of Chinese railroad workers
Mestizos, blend of American Indians and Spanish, most of them living in poverty
many blacks from the West Indies, Jamaica, or Barbados who worked on the canal in early 1900s
many other European, East Asian, and Middle Eastern countries represented in the population

Geography
includes more than 1,500 islands
heavy rainfall, tropical
The Pacific and Caribbean coasts are at sea level.
Pacific coasts have mudflats at low tide.
Mountains run through the middle of Panama like a spine.
longest mountain range called the Cordillera Central
land bridge between Central and South America
country is 480 miles long, 30 to 75 miles wide
Panama shaped like an "S" lying down
long, narrow isthmus called the Isthmus of Panama
highest elevation—Barú Volcano at 11,401 feet
separates Pacific Ocean from the Caribbean Sea and on to the Atlantic Ocean

⇨ **Exposition: The Basics**, Skill 8, p. 82: *Answers will vary.*

⇨ **Exposition: The Basics**, Skill 9, p. 84: *Answers will vary. Here are two possibilities:*

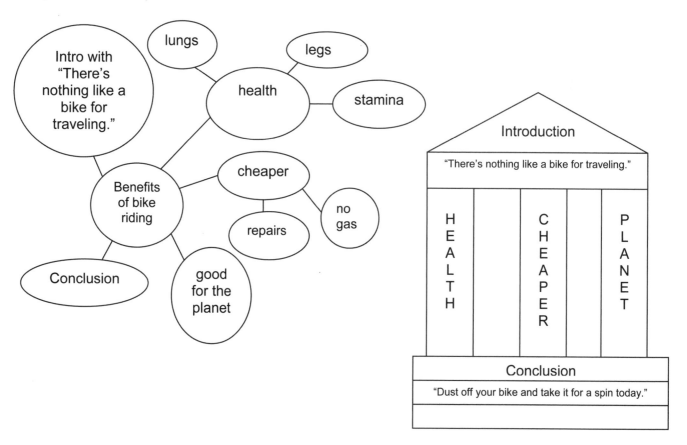

⇨ **Exposition: The Basics**, Skill 10, p. 85:

12, 3	At some point in this process, you have to begin to write. Yes, you do.	IP,IP
13	Putting words down on paper can be the most frustrating part of writing.	(D,D)
10	Don't begin at the beginning if you don't want to! You may write the body	D
19	first, and you may write the introduction and the conclusion last if you like.	IMP
	Remember to turn off your internal editor that tells you how stupid your first	CS
16, 9	sentence is. You can always go back and fix things later!	
	If you were to gather the reports of three friends and read them, you would	IMP, VV
	know which friend wrote which report, even if the names were left off the	
30, 1	papers. How? By the way they use their words and sentences, and by the way	
18, 7	they say things on paper. Your own style is just as distinctive. You have a	IP (D), I
10	certain way, a certain pattern, of writing.	F, D

⇨ **Exposition: The Basics**, Skill 11, pp. 87,88: *Answers will vary. Here are some possibilities:*

Despite what some scientists believe, dinosaurs and men did live on the earth at the same time.

1) Corduroy roads were tricky, 2) Sometimes the colonists built corduroy roads, or 3) Colonial roads were of poor quality.

⇨ **Exposition: The Basics**, Skill 12, pp. 90,91:

Transition sentences:
1. When they arrived in China, they met their new commander.
2. Tex Hill was one of them.
3. Although he was such a surprisingly first-rate pilot, there were still many other great pilots.
4. Our bombers ended up smashingly knocking Japan out of the war in the skies.

The original transition sentence for the first set of paragraphs from *First Steps in the History of Our Country* is this: *"Although the land was for the most part unproductive, the waters were wonderfully full of fish."* Any sentence that leads the reader from the idea of the unproductive land to the idea of lots of fish is acceptable.

The original transition sentence for the second set of paragraphs is this: *"Why, then, should the boys and girls of the United States study the story of this almost unknown man?"* Any sentence that leads the reader to wonder why we study John Cabot is acceptable.

⇨ **Exposition: The Basics**, Skill 13, p. 93: *Answers will vary. Here are some possibilities:*

Dexter Foxx admits in *Wild Fowl I Have Known* (13), "Chicken, duck, goose, pheasant—each has its own delicate taste. I would not turn up my pointed snout at any of these delicious treats."

According to Dexter Foxx at www.wildfowl.com, "Wild turkeys, though the hardest to run down, are the most succulent creatures for a holiday feast."

⇨ **Exposition: The Basics**, Skill 14, p. 95: *Answers will vary.*

⇨ **Exposition: The Basics**, Skill 15, p. 97: *Answers will vary.*

➔   **A Biography**, Skill 1, pp. 99-101:

_1_ Sir James Barrie (*Peter Pan*)   _8_ Michelangelo
_5_ Beverly Cleary (*Ramona* books)   _9_ Walt Disney
_6_ Theodor Geisel (Dr. Seuss)   _3_ Helen Keller
_10_ Abraham Lincoln   _7_ Martin Luther
_4_ J. C. Penney   _2_ George Washington

1. How many of these biographies begin with the person's birth? *Only one*
2. Why is her birth mentioned? *Because we know her as deaf, mute, and blind. It is interesting to know that she was not born that way; we are more curious about her because of the first sentence.*
3. Some of these biographies begin with a hint about how the person became famous. Why is that a good way to start a biography? *It makes us curious about the person. We may know his or her achievements, but we might not know how he or she got there.*

⇨   **A Biography**, Skill 2, pp. 103,104: *Answers will vary.*

⇨   **A Biography**, Skill 3, pp. 105-107: *Answers will vary.*

⇨   **A Biography**, Skill 4, p. 109: *Answers will vary.*

➔   **A Book Report**, Skill 1, pp. 112-114: *Answers will vary.*

⇨   **A Book Report**, Skill 2, pp. 116,117: *Answers will vary.*

⇨   **A Book Report**, Skill 3, p. 119: *Answers will vary.*

⇨   **A Book Report**, Skill 5, p. 126:

1. Did this student follow the suggested paragraphs? *Yes*
2. Do you want to read this book? *Personal opinion*

➔   **A Book Response**, Skill 1, p. 130: *Answers will vary.*

⇨   **A Book Response**, Skill 2, p. 133: *Answers will vary.*

➜ **A Newspaper Article**, Skill 1, pp.136,137:

1. Fact	4. O	7. Fact	10. Fact	13. O
2. O	5. O	8. O	11. Fact	
3. Fact	6. O	9. O	12. Fact	

⇨ **A Newspaper Article**, Skill 2, p. 139: *Answers will vary.*

⇨ **A Newspaper Article**, Skill 3, p. 141:

      Where   What

MOJAVE, Calif. (AP) –An ungainly-looking rocket plane punched through the earth's

                        When   Why (or What)

atmosphere and then glided home to a desert landing Monday in history's first privately financed

manned spaceflight – a voyage that could hasten the day when the final frontier is opened up to

              Who   How   Where again

paying customers. Pilot Mike Melvill took SpaceShipOne 62.2 miles above Earth, just a little more

than 400 feet above the distance considered to be the boundary of space.

⇨ **A Newspaper Article**, Skill 4, p. 142: *Answers will vary.*

⇨ **A Newspaper Article**, Skill 5, pp. 143,144:

1. **Who** did it? *God*
2. **What** did he do? *Created a man and then a woman*
3. **When** did he do it? *On the sixth day*
4. **Where** did he do it? *The man—outside Eden; the woman—inside the Garden of Eden*
5. **Why** did he do it? *More research is needed.*
6. **How** did he do it? *The man—from the dust of the ground; the woman—from the man's rib.*

⇨ **A Newspaper Article**, Skill 6, p. 147: *Answers will vary. Here are some possibilities:*

1. Mark Twain admitted in *Roughing It*, "I was young and ignorant, and I envied my brother."
2. According to http://www.canalmuseum.com/, a great Internet site about the Panama Canal, "A ship traveling from New York to San Francisco can save 7,872 miles using the Panama Canal instead of going around South America."
(or According to www.canalmuseum.com/, a great…)
3. C.S. Lewis, author of *The Lion, the Witch, and the Wardrobe,* has credited the creation of the faun Mr. Tumnus to a dream he had in his teens.

4. The 13-year-old earthquake survivor Maritza Ruiz recounted, "The ground was rolling under my feet. I felt like I was on a boat."

➡ **A How-to**, Skill 1, p. 150: *Answers will vary.*

⇨ **A How-to**, Skill 2, p. 151:

1. Could you make a peanut butter and jelly sandwich from their list? *Personal opinion*
2. Add any steps they left out. *Wash your hands before beginning.*
3. If you wanted to tell your readers some fun things to add to a peanut butter sandwich (other than jelly), where would you add that information? *Most likely after item 5 or 6*
4. Based on the order and completeness of their list, what grade would you give these students? *Personal opinion*

⇨ **A How-to**, Skill 3, p. 153: *Answers will vary.*

⇨ **A How-to**, Skill 4, p. 154,156:

How to Make Homemade Chalk

You will need the following items: an empty toilet paper tube, 1¼ cups plaster of Paris, waxed paper, a disposable container (such as a 15 oz. or larger margarine tub), a plastic spoon, ½ cup water, and, finally, tempera paint.
     1. <u>First</u>, line the inside of your toilet paper tube with waxed paper and set the tube upright on another sheet of waxed paper. 2. <u>Next</u>, make the plaster. Mix together the water and plaster of Paris in the disposable container. 3. <u>When the mixture is smooth,</u> add several spoonfuls of paint until you get the color you like. (I used six spoonfuls of yellow paint and three spoonfuls of red paint to make the color orange.) 4. <u>After you've completed that</u>, use a plastic spoon to put the plaster in the tube. 5. Gently tap the tube to remove any air bubbles.
     6. <u>When you are done</u>, throw away the container and the spoon.   Be careful not to get any plaster down your sink because it will dry and clog up your pipes!
     <u>After twenty-four hours</u>, the plaster should be dry. 7. Carefully peel away the tube from the chalk and take the chalk out of the waxed paper.
     → Have fun drawing!

1. Reread the list on the previous page. Does this writer leave out anything? *An introductory paragraph*
2. What does he do well? *Lists the ingredients, goes step by step, uses transition phrases, and tells you what to do with the chalk.*
3. Based on what you know about a how-to, what grade would you give him? *Personal opinion*

⇨ **A How-to**, Skill 5, p. 158:

These words should be underlined: 1. <u>Wash</u>, 2. <u>Preheat</u>, 3. <u>Get</u>, 4. <u>Gather</u>, 5. <u>Pour</u>, 6. <u>Measure and pour</u>, 7. <u>Add</u>, 8. <u>Turn</u>, 9. <u>Pour</u>, 10. <u>Bake</u>, 11. <u>Ice,</u> 12. <u>Cut and enjoy</u>.

➜ **Compare and Contrast**, Skill 1, p. 162: *Answers will vary.*

⇨ **Compare and Contrast**, Skill 2, p. 163: *Answers will vary.*

⇨ **Compare and Contrast**, Skill 3, pp. 164,165:

1. Which does the author like better: the woods or the sea? *The sea*
2. Which do you like best? Why? *Personal opinion*
3. Which does she mention first? *The woods*
4. Which does she mention last? *The sea*

1. woods   (don't like as much)
2. sea   (like)
3. sea   (like)
4. woods, sea   (don't like as much, like)
5. woods, sea   (don't like as much, like)

⇨ **Compare and Contrast**, Skill 4, pp. 166,167: *Answers will vary.*

⇨ **Compare and Contrast**, Skill 5, p. 170:

1. Write the sentence that is the thesis statement in "Cats Win": *I prefer the cat.*
2. List the **similarities** between cats and dogs (according to the writer): *They're both four-footed, furry animals, and they both are pets.*
List the **differences**: *1) Cats are clean and can bathe themselves/Dogs are dirty and have to have someone bathe them, 2) Cats are smart/Dogs are stupid, and 3) Cats are polite/Dogs are out of control.*
3. Do you agree with the writer of "Cats Win"? *Personal opinion*

⇨ **Compare and Contrast**, Skill 6, pp. 171,172:

1. Which dog does he mention first? *Winnie*
2. Which dog does he mention last? *Beau*
3. Which does he like more? *Beau*
4. What are his three points, which become areas of contrast for the two dogs? *1) Beau is very kind, 2) Beau can do many tricks, and 3) Beau is an obedient dog.*
5. In paragraph two, what does he leave out? *He mentioned Beau, but he didn't contrast him with Winnie.*
6. Which dog would you rather have? *Personal opinion*
7. Based on your knowledge of compare-and-contrast papers, what grade would you give this student? *Personal opinion*

➜ **Description**, Skill 1, p. 176: *Answers will vary.*

⇨ **Description**, Skill 2, p. 177: *Answers will vary.*

⇨ **Description**, Skill 3, pp. 178,179: *Answers will vary.*

⇨ **Description**, Skill 4, p. 180: *Answers will vary. Here is one example (167 words):*

My sister Beth and I glanced out the kitchen window and saw a swirling, black tornado rushing toward us! We grabbed our little brother Marcos and ran to our old, beat-up Chevy truck. Beth pulled the door open, and we jumped in. Our plan was to outrun the tornado. All of us were so frightened, especially when we remembered that it's foolish to try to outrun a tornado. I decided we should hide in a closet under the stairs, so we pulled Marcos from the truck, ran to the house, and jammed ourselves into the tiny closet. Beth slammed the door closed and shut us in. I could feel all of us shivering from fright. Then we heard that awful train sound. I heard the house moan and felt it vibrate around me. Suddenly, there was complete silence. Beth and I peeked out of the closet and stared at what was left of our house. The kitchen was gone! Now I won't have to wash the dishes!

⇨ **Description**, Skill 5, p. 181: *Answers will vary.*

⇨ **Description**, Skill 6, p. 182: *Answers will vary.*

⇨ **Description**, Skill 7, p. 183: *Answers will vary.*

⇨ **Description**, Skill 8, p. 184: *Answers will vary.*

⇨ **Description**, Skill 9, p. 185:

1. Which sense does he use the most? *Hearing, which is appropriate for an orchestra room.*
2. What other senses does he use? *Seeing, feeling*
3. Underline his two similes. *I can feel my body shivering like a cat in the strong wind…, …hop into the van like a kangaroo.*
4. Put an X next to his metaphor. *Mrs. Goldman is a ballerina dancing on the conducting platform.*

⇨ **Description**, Skill 10, pp. 187,188:

1. What is the direction of the spatial description? *Head to foot*
2. Underline the two similes he used to describe the man. *…his arms, thick with muscles, looked like the arms of a great black bear. His legs were as nimble and quick as a mountain goat's.*

1. What do you think she heard in the forest? *Personal opinion and imagination*
2. What kind of a girl is she? *Light, happy, mysterious*
3. What direction is the spatial description? *Head to knees*

4. Underline her simile. *…like twin vines…*

5. **Assonance** is repeating a vowel sound on the insides of words in a row. Edgar Allan Poe uses *assonance* in his poem "The Bells": "m<u>o</u>lten-g<u>o</u>lden n<u>o</u>tes." Where does the writer of this paragraph use assonance? *H<u>u</u>ng, sw<u>u</u>ng*

⇨ **Description**, Skill 11, p. 189:

1. In what direction is the description? *Boots to hair*
2. Do you know what color her hair and eyes are? *No*
3. Underline the simile. *…steam rose from the back of her rain-soaked jacket like morning fog on a river.*
4. What are your impressions of this person? *Personal opinion that might be changed by the last line*
5. What senses were used? *Sight, smell, touch*

⇨ **Description**, Skill 12, pp. 190,191:

Movement: *crowds of people pushing*, *huge wooden-wheeled carts streamed*, *long caravans bound*, and *ships that sailed*

Sight: crowds of people, carts, caravans, sacks and boxes, minstrels, merchants
Sound: people shouting, minstrels singing, merchants advertising
Smell: none
Taste: none
Touch: none

1. What is the direction of the spatial description? *Top to bottom (from the canopy of the trees to the ground)*
2. What is moving? *Milo and his friends ran. The sunlight leaped, slid, and dropped.*
3. Would you like to be in that place with Milo? Explain. *Personal opinion*
4. **Alliteration** is a series of words beginning with the same sound. Edgar Allan Poe used *alliteration* in his poem "The Bells": "What a <u>t</u>ale of <u>t</u>error, now their <u>t</u>urbulency <u>t</u>ells!" Where is the alliteration in this paragraph about Milo and the woods? *<u>L</u>eaped <u>l</u>ightly from <u>l</u>eaf to <u>l</u>eaf*

⇨ **Description**, Skill 13, p. 192: *Answers will vary.*

⇨ **Description**, Skill 14, p. 193: *Answers will vary.*

⇨ **Description**, Skill 15, p. 194: *Answers will vary.*

➔ **Narration (Storytelling)**, Skill 1, p. 196: *Answers will vary.*

⇨ **Narration**, Skill 2, p. 197,198:

1. There was a boy called Eustace Clarence Scrubb, and he almost deserved it. (*Voyage of the Dawn Treader* by C. S. Lewis)
2. It was a dull autumn day and Pole was crying behind the gym. (*The Silver Chair* by C.S. Lewis)
3. Marley was dead: to begin with. (*A Christmas Carol* by Charles Dickens)
4. All children, except one, grow up. (*Peter Pan* by Sir James Barrie)
5. There was once upon a time…
       "A king!" my little readers will instantly exclaim.
       No, children, you are wrong. There was once upon a time a piece of wood.
(*Pinocchio* by C. Collodi)
6. "Where's Papa going with that ax?" said Fern to her mother as they were setting the table for breakfast. (*Charlotte's Web* by E. B. White)

⇨ **Narration**, Skill 3, p. 199: *Answers will vary.*

⇨ **Narration**, Skill 4, p. 201: A*nswers will vary.*

⇨ **Narration**, Skill 5, p. 202: *Answers will vary.*

⇨ **Narration**, Skill 6, p. 203: *Answers will vary.*

⇨ **Narration**, Skill 7, p. 204: *Answers will vary.*

⇨ **Narration**, Skill 8, pp. 206,207:

3____1. His children, too, were as ragged and wild as if they belonged to nobody. His son Rip, an urchin begotten in his own likeness, promised to inherit the habits, with the old clothes, of his father. (*Rip Van Winkle* by Washington Irving)

1____2. For <u>my</u> part, <u>I</u> cannot say that <u>my</u> reflections were very agreeable. <u>I</u> knew that <u>we</u> were on an island, for Jack had said so, but whether it was inhabited or not <u>I</u> did not know. (*The Coral Island* by R. M. Ballantyne)

1____3. After darkly looking at his leg and at <u>me</u> several times, he came closer to <u>my</u> tombstone, took <u>me</u> by both arms, and tilted <u>me</u> back as far as he could hold <u>me</u>; so that his eyes looked most powerfully down into <u>mine</u>, and <u>mine</u> looked most helplessly up into his. (*Great Expectations* by Charles Dickens)

3____4. A few minutes later the little Prince of Wales was garlanded with Tom's fluttering odds and ends, and the little Prince of Pauperdom was tricked out in the gaudy plumage of royalty. (*The Prince and the Pauper* by Mark Twain)

3____5. She had been lying awake turning from side to side for about an hour, when suddenly something made her sit up in bed and turn her head toward the door listening. She listened and she listened. (*The Secret Garden* by Frances Hodgson Burnett)

<u>3</u>   6. His sobs woke Wendy, and she sat up in bed. She was not alarmed to see a stranger crying on the nursery floor; she was only pleasantly interested. (*Peter Pan* by Sir James Barrie)

<u>1</u>   7. You may fancy the terror <u>I</u> was in! <u>I</u> should have leaped out and run for it, if <u>I</u> had found the strength; but <u>my</u> limbs and heart alike misgave <u>me</u>. (*Treasure Island* by Robert Louis Stevenson)

<u>1</u>   8. But the next event to be related is terrible indeed. Its very memory, even now, makes <u>my</u> soul shudder and <u>my</u> blood run cold. (*Journey to the Center of the Earth* by Jules Verne)

<u>1</u>   9. The noise at night would have been annoying to <u>me</u> ordinarily, but <u>I</u> didn't mind it in the present circumstances, because it kept <u>me</u> from hearing the quacks detaching legs and arms from the day's cripples. (*A Connecticut Yankee in King Arthur's Court* by Mark Twain)

<u>3</u>   10. Two of the strongest monkeys caught Mowgli under the arms and swung off with him through the tree-tops, twenty feet at a bound. (*The Jungle Book* by Rudyard Kipling)

⇨ **Narration**, Skill 9, p. 209: *Answers will vary.* Answer to text on p. 208: *third-person limited.*

⇨ **Narration**, Skill 10, p. 210: *Answers will vary.*

⇨ **Narration**, Skill 11, pp. 211,212: *Answers will vary.*

⇨ **Narration**, Skill 12, p. 214:

1. What did the dialogue tell you about the plot? *There is trouble brewing between England and Scotland.*
2. What did the dialogue tell you about the characters? *Duncan is brother to the man; Duncan is a Scotsman and the others are in England; the man and his wife are religious; the human girl thinks the dwarf is ugly.*
3. What point of view (POV) is it written in? *First person*
4. From whose POV is it written? *From the POV of the dwarf*
5. <u>Underline</u> the dialogue (spoken words) and notice the good balance this student has between dialogue and narration:
<u>"Peter, the door!"</u>
<u>"Why are ye here, brother Duncan, at so late a time, and who are those men 'round the horses?"</u>
<u>"Why I be here is to be answered at once if ye let me in."</u>
<u>"Brother, I am come to request…. So, what think ye, my brother?"</u>
<u>"What say ye, Eliza?"</u>
<u>"Have ye any leaning from the Lord? If so, ye may go."</u>

"I do have a leaning from God to go."
"My consent is given, then. Shall we prepare?"
"Why, Miss Adelheid! Ye know ye aren't to scream so, much less at a visitor."
"Father, kill that thing!"

⇨   **Narration**, Skill 13, p. 215: *Answers will vary.*

⇨   **Narration**, Skill 14, p. 217: *Answers will vary.*

⇨   **Narration**, Skill 15, p. 218: *Answers will vary. Here is a possible moral:* Don't attend a picnic with a fox, especially if you're a chicken.

⇨   **Narration**, Skill 16, p. 219: *Answers will vary.*

⇨   **Narration**, Skill 17, p. 220: *1) three chickens, 2) fox throws the Frisbee three times, 3) chickens retrieve it three times, 4) fox digs three holes.*
Other patterns of three: *Answers will vary.*

⇨   **Narration**, Skill 18, pp. 221,222:
Pattern of 3: *Three animals—the buck, the rabbit, and the squirrel, each animal a size smaller*

⇨   **Narration**, Skill 19, p. 224: *Answers will vary.*

➜   **Poetry**, Skill 1, p. 225: *Answers will vary.*

⇨   **Poetry**, Skill 2, p. 226: *Answers will vary.*

⇨   **Poetry**, Skill 3, p. 228: *Answers will vary.*

⇨   **Poetry**, Skill 4, p. 229: *Answers will vary.*

⇨ **Poetry**, Skill 5, p. 230:

My <u>J</u>esus, I <u>love</u> Thee, I <u>know</u> Thou art <u>mine</u>.   ___A___
For <u>Thee</u> all the <u>fo</u>llies of <u>sin</u> I re<u>sign</u>.   ___A___
My <u>gr</u>acious Red<u>ee</u>mer, my <u>S</u>avior art <u>Thou.</u>   ___B___
If <u>ev</u>er I <u>l</u>oved Thee, my <u>J</u>esus, 'tis <u>now</u>.   ___B___

A<u>ma</u>zing <u>grace</u>! How <u>sweet</u> the <u>sound</u>   ___A___
That <u>saved</u> a <u>wretch</u> like <u>me</u>!   ___B___
I <u>once</u> was <u>lost</u> but <u>now</u> am <u>found</u>,   ___A___
Was <u>blind</u> but <u>now</u> I <u>see</u>.   ___B___

⇨ **Poetry**, Skill 6, p. 232: *Answers will vary.*

⇨ **Poetry**, Skill 7, p. 233: *Answers will vary.*

NOTES

NOTES

NOTES

NOTES

NOTES

NOTES

NOTES